Unlocking the Digital Code:
A Guide to Strategically Master Social Media Marketing

Professor Jen Riley

DEDICATION

For Trinity, Aaron, Gene and Bella- may this book be a reminder that you can achieve anything you set your mind towards and that every goal is completed by taking just one step at a time.

To all those that have been my supporters in all ventures over the years: Mom, Dad, Jessica, Mrs. Deborah, Kae, Mika, Byrd & Harv, thank you! Thanks to my fellow Petrels (too many to list you all), my fellow Toastmasters, former professors (Chandler & V. Kumar) students and mentees, and everyone else who has supported me. Special thanks to Arvisse and Malia and all the PAC clients, especially ChopArt and The Email Specialist!

The motivation and encouragement pushing me to keep going has meant the world and inspired me to never, ever give up.

Thank You!

CONTENTS

INTRODUCTION

Social. Media. Two very simple words that have made a massive impact on business and changed the scope of both human interaction and communication as we know it. On a personal level, social media connects users with their friends, allows them to stalk their ex or next, and is a convenient way to waste time at work. Outside of personal use, social media also helps businesses both large and small. In this day and age, I think it's safe to say most business owners see the legitimacy and strength social media *can* bring a company or organization and they *might* even agree marketing this way is effective. However, it has taken business owners and marketers a long time to find a semi-mutual understanding and reach the conclusion that social media is not only here to stay, but also a good idea.

While we might not all agree on its hierarchy of importance in the marketing equation, most business owners and marketers alike share the stance that social media is a powerful method to reach customers and is growing as a crucial part of the marketing mix. There are still devout traditional marketers that believe there is no return on time and money invested in social media. I must disagree with that opinion but admit I agree it is *not* the magic answer to all business plans. Social media will <u>not</u> solve all your business needs and generating an idea with the intention to *"post on Facebook"* as your marketing strategy will **not** make you an overnight billionaire. You may laugh, but I have had many clients (both young and old) think that would be the case.

Marketing still takes a lot of work, and I would even go a step further to say social media demands even more work than other means of reaching your target audience. It is crucial that all readers understand traditional marketing is still needed and social media is a means to elevate your marketing message. You cannot take the principles suggested in this book and abandon all other marketing. You can, however, integrate the principles written here and use them to enhance your overall marketing plan.

The split is not as simple as traditional marketing versus "new age" or digital marketing. Now we have the segmentation of online marketing versus offline marketing. Because consumers now have the power to photograph or record anything with little to no effort and share via the internet, a lot of the offline marketing still has a presence online.

Online *or* Digital Marketing has a vast footprint and is mirrored in offline marketing as well. Beyond social media, other types of digital marketing methods include websites, email marketing, Google AdWords, Google Analytics, blogging, banner ads/pop-up ads, Search Engine Optimization (SEO), Search Engine Marketing (SEM), podcasts, webinars, white papers, case studies, E-books, online classes, and online forums / discussion boards. This is a lot, I know, but you are not required to do them all. The beautiful part of being able to market online in abundance is the ability for all of these initiatives to work together. There are no silos online; if you do two, five, or all of these mediums, they will work together. Be mindful not to launch everything just to say you have. It is hard to manage them all without the proper resources in place and it is very important to be successful in one rather than mediocre in ten. This is why we must be purposeful and intentional when developing a brand presence on any digital marketing platform, more specifically, on any social media platform. When executed well, whichever strategic resource(s) a company chooses from the list above, the purposeful selection will yield more results than the popular one will.

This book is built to educate the small business owner, nonprofit leader, and entrepreneurial community to the benefits of social media marketing. The techniques here are specifically designed to teach effective use of social media although you will see overlap with digital marketing at large and inclusion of offline initiatives. Your mission while reading this book is to develop a social media marketing campaign of your choice. Follow the prompts throughout the book to help you keep track and develop your campaign, start to finish. Let's get started!

CHAPTER 1: CAMPAIGN 411

Learning Objectives:

I.   Identify needed elements of a social media campaign
II. Determine details of your campaign target audience
III. Analyze the brand's Strengths, Weaknesses, Opportunities and Threats (SWOT Analysis)
IV. Identify SMART goals and objectives for campaign

As discussed in the introduction, this book addresses Social Media Marketing from the aspect of building campaigns. Regardless of whether you are planning an event you want to sell-out, fundraising for your nonprofit organization, or creating an active online presence for your small business, social media strategies are all about campaigns. Campaigns provide structure and a concept around which you build content. Without them, the process can become very monotonous and redundant. Campaigns prevent unwanted repetition and give you something to support.

Campaign details are crucial to getting started when using social media to market your small business or nonprofit organization. No decisions can be made or plans executed without knowing the "who, where, what, why, and how" of your campaign.

We shall begin with the 'who'. Learning your target audience can be an entire book on its own. Although a major element of the campaign, to stay on track, let's only review the highlights.

[1]

Every marketing initiative should have a target audience. This target audience will tell you who your entire campaign is geared toward. All decisions are made based on the persona of this group of people. After all, they are the ones you want to buy your service, product or attend your event. Now, I know what you're thinking: "I want everyone to buy my product, so obviously my target audience is everyone!"

NO!

"Everyone" cannot, I repeat, *CANNOT* be a true target audience. There are multiple issues this stance invites. First, marketing to "everyone" requires quite a hefty budget. Second, let's say your product is an innovative baby bottle, does "everyone" have babies? No, they do not. What about customized NFL team blankets? Is "everyone" a football fan? No, they are not. How about a livestream camera that allows you to see and interact with your pet wherever you are? How would individuals without pets use that product?

Apple has done an exceptional job at infiltrating iPhones into homes across America, but it was not always that way. They had to start with innovators, people who understood and loved technology, then the others followed as it became more mainstream. Their primary target audience still isn't "everyone" because they have to please their primary following- the Apple loyalists. Some individuals that are "too techy" don't like the limitations the OS places on the device so they prefer Android. Every product or service has a group of people that is the "right fit", just like every job is not for every worker. Defining your target audience as "everyone" strains the budget by casting the net way too wide and prevents the crafting of messages optimized for a specific group. We will discuss that further in a later chapter.

To establish a successful target audience, you need to have a few things:
- Age range
- Demographic details
- Geographic details
- Income level or idea of discretionary funds
- Education level
- Interests

Some clients have asked, "Are all of these elements required to define my target audience?" The short answer is no. But the more important answer is, the more you understand your target audience the more successful your marketing initiatives will be. At this stage, most students are still a little unclear. If you need a little more direction, hopefully these examples will help:

Example A: my target audience is men, women and children. Nope, that is just another way to say everyone.

Example B: my target audience is men because women do not usually work in construction. I will limit the age from 18-40 because there is extreme strain on your body so most older men stop working in the field at an older age and this product is purely for those working onsite daily, not management. Finally, I won't clarify geographic location, education level, demographics, or interests because there is no consistency to race, location or education level when reviewing the data of current customers. Interests are not something we track since this is a work-related product.

Example C: my target audience is the millennial generation group, aka young adults (it is important to be mindful with descriptions and to be as finite as possible to not leave descriptors to interpretation of others, technically millennials is a much wider group than the young professional), age 22-35 at the time of the product launch. Very tech-savvy, with college educations or in college currently but placing high value on being a trendsetter among their friends and on the cutting edge of technology. This group of consumers is both male and female and primarily spends money on personal interests and recreation past their begrudged obligations like student loans. They see technology not only as a necessity but also a special treat to ease the sense of adulthood.

If you need more help defining your target audience, email info@PhoenixArisingConsulting.com for a consultation, be sure to mention this book to waive the fee for the first 15min.

Now that we have thought about who our target customers are, and hopefully have a primary and secondary target audience identified, let's talk about the 'where'. All social media sites are **not** created equal, and although a lot of them have similar features, each one has distinct characteristics and functionality that causes certain ones to stand out, based on user needs. The best way to ensure you are matching your audience with the right network is research.

During your research of social networks you must consider:
1. The features you want to help market your business and whether they exist on the platform network of choice.
2. Your target audience. You cannot market to a group that is not using the platform where you populate all of your information.

For example, if I have a new app that translates text into a language from Star Wars, a very specific type of person would be interested in that, i.e., a specific target audience. Generally we would go to Google+ for something like that because coders, developers, and video gamers that enjoy things like Star Wars are often found there. Would they also be on SnapChat, taking selfies and videos of themselves? Not so much.

Let's have another example. The majority of people are on Facebook (when this book was written), so if your product or service has a general audience *or* you are unsure where your audience is online, Facebook is the best bet. They also offer the most features for a business or brand; you are able to use their specific services to market to the public. When social media sites are created, they are built entirely for the purpose of the consumer. They attract users to prove the worth of the network to advertisers, and then, and only then, do they start creating and offering things for a brand (business or organization). To date, Facebook has the most business-friendly features out of any social media platform, including LinkedIn. They continue to assess the landscape and how marketers can use the platform to reach target audiences, thereby increasing marketers' loyalty to the platform.

One last example. If you are targeting teens, you want to go to the most popular, and often the newest, platform. Teens tend to migrate away from the more well-established social media sites that have a business component. Google is your friend during this process. Because the stats and trends change, we cannot successfully give you a bunch of scenarios to help you decide and then promise it will remain factual for the next 16 years or days. We can, however, give you strategies to address any social site regardless of the changes over time. Marketing using social media with a strategy changes the way you look at each site and allows you to see the utility past that funny cat video or other applications for the personal user landscape.

Now that we know the 'who' and the 'where', it's time to conquer the 'what, why, and how'. The rest of the book includes information on these three areas. But to get started with the 'what', we first have to talk a little bit about vision and analysis.

Someone once said, "To know where you are going, you have to know where you have been." A company's mission and vision statements must align with everything it does online, especially in social media. If you are marketing a business one way and have successfully converted that viewer from a social platform to your website and upon arrival the tone of the company is drastically different, it will leave a poor taste in their mouth and have the brand appear inauthentic. Inconsistencies of "voice" can waste a lot of time and resources when building an online brand. Branding is so much more than colors and a logo. It's an experience. Customers love social media because they get to know the brand. That brand starts with the mission statement and the vision, which is why alignment is so crucial.

The other needed piece to this part of the puzzle is analysis. At Phoenix Arising Consulting (PAC), we recommend a SWOT Analysis at the start of any project, big or little. Or every Monday, whichever comes first (That's just a joke, mainly for my students as they grew loathsome of my emphasis on this type of review). Many business professionals are familiar with the SWOT, but for those that need a refresher, you assess the Strengths, Weaknesses, Opportunities and Threats (SWOT) of any given situation. A SWOT Analysis can be done from a high level point-of-view, but can also be applied to anything that you want or need to review and assess to strategically improve.

The reason we preach this practice very heavily to clients is to encourage self-reflection. As a consulting firm, we can enter any situation and provide feedback and suggestions for improvement, but if a client can objectively evaluate with progress in mind, the solutions we build would be so much stronger. A solution based on a client's assessment of their strengths, weaknesses, threats, and opportunities is likely to be more effective even quicker than that of an outside party. Know your weaknesses to build them stronger, avoid threats and take advantage of the opportunities.

You might wonder why this matters for social media. Well, whether you are starting from scratch at the beginning of your social journey or you are in the midst but not well-established with a strong and engaged following, or you are a veteran and have been doing it since before Facebook offered a business page, you will always have something to put in each of these categories.

Here is an example of a social media specific SWOT analysis:

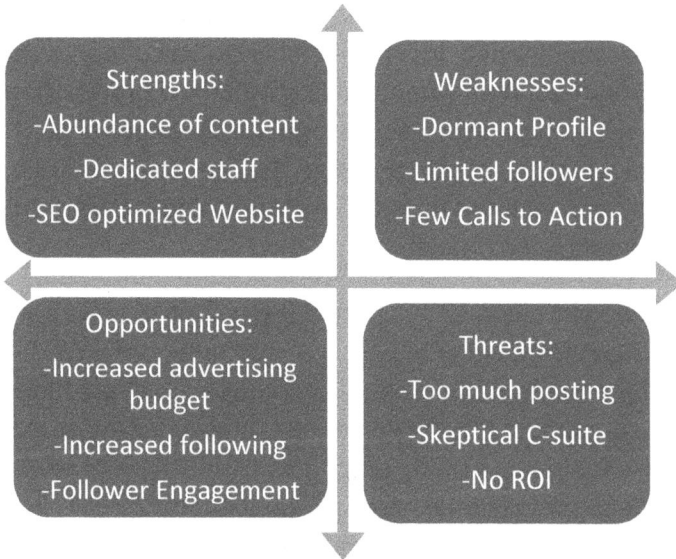

Strengths:	Weaknesses:
-Abundance of content	-Dormant Profile
-Dedicated staff	-Limited followers
-SEO optimized Website	-Few Calls to Action
Opportunities:	Threats:
-Increased advertising budget	-Too much posting
-Increased following	-Skeptical C-suite
-Follower Engagement	-No ROI

Before you start your campaign, conduct a new analysis, even if your company does one every quarter. This time, limit the scope of your SWOT and just consider your social media presence. Do you have a lot of followers? Are your profiles suffering from a lack of page activity, from either the users or you as the admin? Or, a very common problem with small business owners, has there only been a message or two since the inception of the page?

As you are asking yourself these questions or brainstorming with the team, place the answers in their respective quadrants. You want to conduct this exercise until you have at least three items in each area and no more than five. If the list gets too long, it will be hard to zero in and focus on turning that weakness into a strength or taking advantage of an opportunity. It is very important to not only be aware but also to not overwhelm yourself or your team. Revisit this practice frequently, and you will find the more intentional you are with activities after, the more you'll see positive shifts and progress made.

After completing the SWOT analysis review, our next step is to address the timeframe of the campaign and establish our campaign focus. It has been my experience that people's perception of developing social media content is that it's an "easy enough" process. Until, of course, the stakes are raised and they are no longer posting for recreational use. Then they don't know what to say, aren't getting the engagement for which they hoped, or the content is just downright repetitive and too sales focused. As my mom would say, content is the meat and potatoes of any social media campaign. But there are three chapters dedicated to building stellar content so we will address that later. For now, however, let's figure out how long this campaign will last and what will be the focus.

First, you might wonder, why do we have to do this as campaigns? Or, what does she mean *campaigns*, I thought this was a book on social strategies? I'm glad you asked. For those of you that have been active in the social arena, you know the challenge of developing content for the same brand or set of brands week after week. Those that are unfamiliar with the process are saved with the campaign theory, as I like to call it. When creating content for a campaign, you have a scope of a few major elements needed to create good content, the who, what, when, and where. Campaigns give you a subject matter for which you can center the content within, an automatic who, what, when, and where. Without that framework, you are playing guessing games and scrambling to find relevant content or neglecting to post entirely until it's too late. At this point, most users conclude that social just isn't right for their business, when really, it simply was not addressed properly.

Just as we are accustomed to from our school days, the calendar year is more digestible when split into sections. Campaigns allow you to split your social media marketing year the same way. Social media campaign durations are run in three, six, nine, and twelve month time periods. You can sync the campaign with your overall marketing calendar or conduct them separately. The parameter of a time and subject eases the content development process to prevent business owners or staff from the "blank stare" moment at the computer.

The campaign overview and objectives serve the purpose of telling marketers during a certain period of time what we are here to market. A specific campaign can also have a slightly different target audience from the overall company. I've found that frequent campaigns run by companies both on and off of social media have a subset of the overall target audience rather than the entire audience as a whole. For example, if this campaign is for a new product, that product might target a new segment. However, if we are doing a general branding campaign to increase brand awareness within the primary target, we have a very clear idea and are promoting on a grander scale.

The time frame selected should correspond with the campaign focus. For example, a brand awareness campaign can be for six months in its entirety but broken in half to focus on two key areas of the business. Let's say you are marketing an event. Let's not choose the three month duration if we can avoid it; there should be at least six months in advance for an event if we are selling tickets and want a high attendance rate.

Although it seems like people won't commit to things in this day and age, best practice indicates that events should have a proper lead time for promotion. But, not all events require this much lead time. A lot of the campaign duration depends on the focus and your target audience. A Halloween haunted house might not require six months of planning and marketing for one specific event. You might choose to go with a three month campaign leading up to the day to coincide with the retailer's decorating. Whereas, if you want people to come to an album release party in the middle of June, no major holiday adjacent, you should start six months in advance.

Our second step is to determine objectives. We must ask a few qualifying questions to select reasonable and realistic objectives. What is it we want to get out of this campaign, the best scenario? Is it increased followers? Visits to the website? Clicks, sales, ticket sales, messages, comments, likes, shares, etc.? This section can be overwhelming; if you have ten objectives, you have too many. Get them all out and marinate on them to identify what is currently the most important to the business. Then, prioritize! But remember, the focus of this campaign is to reach the objectives, so be realistic. They can be general, however - specificity is for the SMART goals, our next step.

We are almost done with the reflective portion of the campaign, but these steps are crucial to the success of the campaign deployment. SMART is an acronym to describe how to generate the most effective goal. You want your goals to be Specific, Measureable, Achievable, Realistic, and Timely. A specific goal will have more details such as, "I want to increase the engagement (viewer's interactions) on each post for our Facebook page," versus an unspecific goal such as, "I want everyone to see all our messages." A measurable goal is key, especially for those of you that desire to consult other brands, manage their profiles for them, or report on social activity and progress.

Measureable assists with the specifics. If you want to increase user engagement on Facebook, select a set percentage, 30% for example, or review how many users see your posts on average and calculate a percentage using that figure. Achievable and realistic work in tandem. To increase a small business Facebook page by 30,000 users might be a tad extreme and out of range or budget for most business owners. But, if you want to increase by 10%, it is more realistic and achievable. Timely is key and works very well with the campaign duration. A goal can be realistic and within a brand's reach and suddenly become past their scope of abilities due to timeliness. If you want to double your audience in three weeks but it took you three years to get to your current point, that's unrealistic based purely on the time constraints.

At this point of the book, you should have your campaign duration, campaign focus, SWOT analysis for your brand, campaign objectives, and SMART Goals. The following Progress Quiz will help you implement the practices taught in this chapter and quizzes will follow at the end of others to keep you on track as well.

Progress Quiz

1. What are the who, why, and what elements of your campaign?
2. How long will your campaign last and will it integrate with any other element of your marketing mix?
3. Do you know where your target audience frequents on social media platforms?
4. What are your brand's SWOT elements?
5. Have you set your SMART Goals and made sure they are Specific, Measureable, Achievable, Realistic, and Timely?

CHAPTER 2: CAMPAIGN PLATFORM SELECTION

Learning Objectives:
  I.   Clarify the target audience specifically for this campaign
  II. Develop a persona for your ideal customer
  III. Match the target audience to specific social media platforms
  IV. Assess various social media platform offerings and benefits
  V.   Select the final campaign platforms based on a compilation of the target audience and the platform offerings

Now that we have gotten started with some crucial questions for the campaign in chapter one, it's time for a nice mix of why and how. We spoke a little about choosing your platforms in the last chapter, but not nearly enough. Let's dive in a bit more. We can apply a 3-step process to select the best platforms for your target audience and campaign.

  1. Clarify Audience
  2. Match target audience to platform
  3. Compare platforms offerings and benefits

Step 1- Clarifying the audience.

Clarifying your target audience area connects with the campaign focus. We reviewed the brand's primary and secondary target audiences in the first chapter, but our social campaign is not limited to that same group. Before we continue, let's clarify the target audience.

Ask yourself (or your team) the following questions:
- Who in the brand's overall target audience cares about this campaign focus?
- Is this for something new or a market we already serve?
- Are we engaging this group differently from how we have done in the past?
- What are this audience's interests outside of my particular product or service?
- What geographic area would I find this type of customer?
- What is their level of education, family size, extra-curricular activities outside of work/school, etc.?

This process aids not only the advertising piece but also the #hashtag and content engagement elements to come later. Now it's time to build a persona for this ideal customer within your campaign-specific target audience.

Building a persona entails developing the ideal person that would purchase your brand product/service or donate to your nonprofit. Answering all the questions listed above, you will begin to learn your target audience for the campaign and be better equipped to craft content and engage them throughout the campaign. A completed persona could look like this:

Name: Jessica (*Does not have to be exact, this practice of naming the persona is simply to keep them separate when working with multiples at the same point or in the same campaign*)

Age: 34
Education: Bachelor's Degree, professional certification
Location: Northeast US
Income: $45,000-$60,000
Family size: single, never married, no kids, 2 cats
Career: Teaching
Professional Associations: Teach for America, Teach USA
Interests: DIY projects, history, home renovations, HGTV
Values: family oriented, goal oriented, honesty, creativity
Extra-curricular Activities: Kickball, Meet-ups, Wine club
Primary Platforms: Pinterest, Facebook, YouTube

Step 2- Matching the target audience to the platform.

Everyone who reads this book is not reading it before they start their social media presence. Your brand could already have a presence and be active on them all. Pinterest, YouTube, Vine, SnapChat, Twitter, LinkedIn, Facebook, Instagram, Google+, Periscope - the list of available platforms goes on and on! Regardless of the platforms where your brand has a presence, a history there does not make it right for your campaign. The campaign we are building here has its own voice, just the same as it can have its own target audience. The brand voice is different, however, but we will address that later as well.

For those of you just starting your social media experience for a brand, I encourage you to not only consider what is right for this campaign but also what is needed for the brand as a whole. A social media platform is a lot of work to maintain, and you do not want to spread your resources and staff too thin trying to be everything to everyone, everywhere.

As we think about our brand's online presence, the type of content we want to post, various promotions we want to run, education of our product or services, and the persona for the person ready, willing and waiting to hear all of those aspects, certain platforms stand out from others. This thought process of matching a campaign to specific platforms makes the content creation element much more digestible and the practice less arduous. That is not to say the same campaign cannot be on multiple platforms, because it can. It simply means understanding a platform and how your target audience interacts with it.

For example, the persona ironed out above, Jessica, loves DIY projects but she also values family. She is on Pinterest for creative, artistic expression and inspiration. Her Facebook page, however, could have funny cat videos and her mini-feed flooded with friends and family, college friends having kids, wine groups, etc. A brand would interact differently with Jessica on each of these platforms but, we could run the same campaign on both, no problem. The content would just look different because of how to end user engages each platform. We will cover aggregates in a later chapter, but the same content formulated differently per platform is the reason to **not** broadcast all social content to all platforms all the time. That would be like talking to a room of 50 students the same way when they are different people and accept information in varying ways.

This step requires a bit of research for your target audience, for not only where they are, but also knowing which profile generally fits what type of target audience. The challenge is how this information changes over time. Instagram can be the hottest thing currently and in two months turn into old news because now SnapChat is the most popular at that point in time. The good news is, just like technology as a company, businesses do not always have to adapt as quickly as users. As you see just a chapter and a half into the book, social media is quite complex so all businesses do not follow the same trends, and I would highly discourage against establishing a presence on a platform purely because of a trend. You will drive yourself bonkers if you do.

Step 3- Compare platform offerings and benefits.

Social media was built for users, first and foremost. The most common business model for social platforms is to build a network with some unique feature and attract a mass audience. Next they leverage their popularity with the users and their time spent (or wasted) on the platform to attract to investors, advertisers and marketers. This segment of the population, the social platform's real target audience, are lured due to the buying power users on the platforms represent.

The creators of the social platform promote this idea that "Your users and potential customers are here so you should be here as well," which is completely valid. For example, if a potential or existing consumer is on Facebook a lot, it makes sense to be there as a business so that they see your content and you stay top of mind. Additionally, if users are spending the majority of their day on the platform, it only makes sense they would use the social network as a place to do research as well. It's said that the majority of consumers learn their behavior from family and look to friends for referrals and references. If this is true, social media is a hotbed of endorsements!

We are in an information age where everything we want to know is generally at our fingertips. By choosing the right platforms, you can help your target audience (and your bottom line) by making the information for your brand readily available where they are. The more a customer has to go out of their way to locate details of a product or service, the more likely they are to get distracted by something else, commonly a competitor, and not convert to a customer.

All social media platforms are not created equal. Users flock to various platforms for two things: the features available and the audience (their friends). Similar to users, businesses should have the same motivations for their presence on platforms. Not all platforms offer a business specific interface, but those that do offer a different set of benefits to a brand or business profile than they do to users. For example, Facebook brand pages (they offer more pages than for a business but what they do all have in common is a brand, so I dub them as this, also previously known as "fan pages") allow users to schedule a post, gather analytics and target specific users. Let's further examine benefits as a whole. Not all of these features are available on every platform, but to date these are the most popular that add a competitive edge to one platform over another:

1. Post scheduling
2. Post editing after publishing
3. Brand page functionality versus general user distinction
4. Advertising
5. Analytics (viewer stats, engagement, demographic, and geographic)
6. Contact information and messaging capabilities
7. Posts including live, clickable links
8. Hashtag enabling
9. User engagement (like, click, comment, share, RT, etc.)
10. Video posting (editing and length varies by platform)
11. Content longevity and lifespan (algorithm)
12. Photo posting (editing and filters)
13. Movable images (GIFs)
14. Trending Topics section
15. Backdating posts
16. Lists, page subscriptions and "follow" options
17. 3rd party integrations

Although a lengthy list of features, these are among many. Some of the above features are restricted to a brand specific profile, whereas others are a natural competitive edge. As a business, you have to assess a platform not only for the audience you are targeting and that frequent the platform, but also from a features perspective. Features change on a weekly basis depending on the platform. Facebook, for instance, has the most features of any social media platform that are available specifically for business profiles. For example, Facebook page admins can edit messages after the post is live, unlike Twitter. If there is a mistake on Twitter, the entire tweet must be deleted resulting in the loss of likes, comments, RTs (ReTweets), and views. Facebook business or brand profiles are also able to specify their target audience, schedule messages for a future date and time and review analytics for the performance of their content. Most of these features are only available on Facebook, and the platform continues to rollout new features.

In this step, you will also need to assess your resources, time, staff, and money to help evaluate which platform makes the most sense for your current stage of marketing development. For example, if advertising is not available, there is no need for that feature. Chapter 8 details team assessment from a management perspective but, from a features angle, if you have a staff of one, a platform offering 3rd party aggregate management **OR** schedule posting is the best choice. After researching platform features that meet business needs, determining your ideal client persona and aligning where customers spend their time online with the features, sync both elements together to select the platform(s) for the campaign.

Progress Quiz
1. Describe your target audience brand persona?
2. What social media platform does your ideal customer frequent?
3. What benefits for a platform are most important to you?
4. What social media platforms meet your business needs?
5. Determine which social media platforms you will use for your campaign.

CHAPTER 3: NAVIGATING SOCIAL AS A BUSINESS

Learning Objectives:
I.   Explore social media navigation as a business
II. Discover fundamentals for developing content calendars
III. Get acquainted with the 80/20 Rule and a content voice

When users heard "advertisers" and "marketers" would be on Facebook, they groaned. Why? Because they are TIRED OF BEING SOLD TO! Information overload is so real that as consumers, we are asked for money at every turn. A commercial on TV, a billboard on the way home, ads on the radio, pop-up ads online, email ads, sale notifications, Geo-targeting, SMS notifications, charities looking for donations - information is *everywhere* and 99% of the information sources want your money. As business owners, we think, "We just need a piece of the pie from enough of our target audience to meet the bottom line." But that is never enough. We want to *grow* the business and that is what leads us to initiatives like social media marketing.

Consumers, however, like information when they are searching for things in the buying process. But their primary goal on social media is connecting to other users. We live in an odd world where people will sit right next to each other but engage more with their phones and friends who aren't in close proximity than they will with someone less than a foot away. As a society, we use social media to connect and converse with friends and family, and to find like-minded thinkers (or debate with non-like-minded thinkers). Users rarely set out or look for connections with businesses; typically social media is a place for entertainment and escape.

Regardless of a user's motives for activating profiles and investing time in social media, their main goal is not usually to have it be another avenue marketers use to sell them on a new product or idea. This concept of why people are on social media connects back to knowing your target audience. Just the other day, I had a conversation with a client about what profile is best for him. He wants businesswomen, but he wants ones that are interested in travel and exploring new cities. First of all, that can be a complex target to reach. Secondly, that type of consumer is on multiple platforms. But, as every platform is different and serves a different purpose to its users, she uses every platform very differently. She might be on LinkedIn as a businesswoman, but when it is time for her to travel she is looking to Facebook, Pinterest, and Instagram for ideas, feedback from friends, family, and possibly other users.

Traditionally, it is said to take seven touches with a potential customer to convert them to a paying client. It can be speculated that seven times is a minimum these days, but social media can also expedite these touches. Now, customers do a lot more research and investigation for themselves rather than taking a company's word. Customers are also extremely active online and will trust other customers before they trust what the company says about themselves, which is often a well-practiced and rehearsed spiel. Review sites like Yelp count on research conducted by users to draw traffic. Potential customers want to know what other customers have said. In that search process, wouldn't it be to your advantage if they kept finding information from your company among the reviews? Yes it would!

Social media is the best way to stay top of mind without constantly selling to people. I like to call it the subliminal selling tool. By being present, consistent, helpful, and interesting, businesses can build a relationship with their audience. Then, once the need arises, that business is top of mind for the customer and it shortens their consumer behavior typical research time. This process, of course, takes time and patience but also consistent content.

Typically, it takes 90 days of consistent content to get people to recognize a brand's presence. An average of over six months to get people to engage and approximately one year to get a return from that avenue. As ironic as it sounds for a real-time, constantly moving arena like social media to have such an extended conversion cycle, it's true. A brand has to build trust, and brands also have to consider the standard sales cycle for their product or service. Big purchases often take longer than small purchases. Big companies have a lot more red tape and approvals that might be met before a purchase than smaller companies or entrepreneurs.

Thinking of this timeline from a content perspective and needing to have a year's worth of topics and information to discuss can be extremely daunting. But, there is a better way. The campaign theory model allows managers a topic that all content can revolve around. By dissecting that long timeline into little sections, we can apply campaigns within that lengthy time period. To this point in the book, we have completed the several steps toward developing campaigns. By now you should have:

1. Completed the assessment of the business including: Establishing a strong understanding of the brand mission statement, target audience, core values and be equipped to align your social campaign to that standard.
2. Conducted a SWOT analysis for current social state or marketing of the business
3. Determined campaign target audience and built a persona for the primary target
4. Identified the campaign duration (3, 6, 9 or 12 month time periods)
5. Established campaign objectives and SMART goals
6. Selected campaign platforms
7. In the next chapter we will brainstorm what type of content is best and possible strategies for content development.

If you have not completed these, I would suggest to take a break from reading to work on these elements before continuing. Now is also a good time to review the steps as a whole to make any changes as you see fit and remind yourself before we move forward. Our next major step is our content calendar. It sounds like a really big step, and we have been taking bite sized progressions toward the end goal of an effective strategy for social media, but you can do this in little steps too.

Building a content calendar is important because it gives our campaign the framework we need to focus on granular levels while maintaining the high-level view we have nurtured in chapters 1-3. Some social media managers (I was one when I first started) will simply have a monthly or quarterly theme. I found that was great, but not enough information or inspiration to motivate the team for interesting and engaging content. For sports fans, a content calendar is your playbook. For the crowd that likes to cook, it is your recipe. This piece of information is developed to keep you on track. It's impractical to refer back to this highly robust campaign proposal time and time again throughout the life of the campaign but an overview like a content calendar gives you the snippet you need to make it to the next step.

There are templates you can use to help (please refer to the resources section). I suggest using Excel if you elect to develop it from scratch. Let's review the steps to building this content calendar; keep in mind, some of the included elements we have not discussed at length yet but will in the following chapters:

1. Assess company needs - is there a particular service we need to promote? A section of our portfolio we want to grow or an introduction of a new product or service? How do our campaign goals and objectives overlap with the needs of the company?
2. Assess what's happening with company - are we in a transition? Is there a sale or promotion that could be leveraged with this campaign?
3. Your calendar length should match the campaign duration but conducted by month. For a three month campaign, you would have three content calendars, one per month.
4. Review traditional marketing plans - what will happen when for the overall marketing of the company during this same time period? Are we launching a commercial, posting a billboard, sending out newsletters etc.?
5. Analyze rest of world at large - what occurrences will happen while this campaign is running? Is it a national holiday? What could distract our target audience that we should be mindful of or consciously include in our plans?
6. Analyze the industry - is this a big time for the industry we are in? For example, the video game industry has a big conference every year called E3. Video game related

companies doing this exercise within the month the conference normally occurs would want to know about it and plan accordingly. Maybe they need to include it in the content calendar in order to have a representative there to live tweet or post a blog right before and after.

7. Establish or review approved #hashtag list - we have not discussed #hashtags in depth yet; that comes in another chapter. But, for this step of your content calendar, you should have a list of approved #hashtags you have researched and can integrate into the previously listed items for the campaign. This is a list that content developers can pull from when crafting social content to support the campaign. They can also include popular hashtags that are not directly related to the subject matter along with company specific ones.

8. Determine a target post frequency - for the platforms selected and the target audience, what frequency do we want to have when posting for this campaign? For example, it is too often to post to Facebook six times in one day but for Twitter, that amount of content is just right.

9. Assign any themes and craft posts - if you have certain days where specific posts should be sent, assign them here. I suggest a weekly view for the month and a more detailed version where you populate the content once crafted.

10. Optimize for target audience and schedule - the final step is reviewing and optimizing the written content to ensure it will reach the target audience as intended. After the content is optimized, including adding in the post-specific hashtags, it is ready for approval and scheduling!

It is easy to get lost in the process between strategizing and content creation. The content calendar provides order and guidance to help content generators stay focused. However, content generation introduces multiple opportunities to be led astray. The last two crucial pieces to understand as a business using social media marketing is your content voice and balance of the 80/20 rule. The content voice is important for consistency. Regardless of how big the team is, if you switch marketing firms or content managers, you don't want your audience to know. Profiles that maintain the same voice have a continuity that makes it appear that the same person is writing the content. Chapter 5 will unpack both of these concepts further but first, let's talk about content types.

CHAPTER 4: CONTENT CREATION PT. I

Learning Objectives:
  I.   Learn the various types of content options on social media
  II.   Identify the best types of content to share per campaign
  III. Explore your brand's content voice

Regardless of what you have heard or which social media platform you choose, there is always one and only ONE constant in all digital marketing - Content is King! Without content, your social media presence (klout) will die. One of the hardest aspects of managing social media platforms, as a business or on behalf of a business, is the continuous generation of content. You can be popular one day, and then stop posting and be forgotten the next. If the content stops, your user engagement also stops. Social media users look for consistency from a brand; they want to know you are authentic but also engaging with them in real-time. Due to this "real-time" requirement, I encourage you not to prepare and schedule all posts ahead of time, but continuously post some "in the moment" messages as well.

Although the "real-time" engagement is the landscape of social, from a business perspective, this also creates a problem. We don't all have budgets to hire someone to manage our profiles 24/7, and imagine how expensive that would be if we did! Even some of the big brands that employ entire departments specifically for social media and have millions in their marketing budget are not always ready and equipped to handle opportunities that arise. The best way to solve this conundrum is a mix of prepared and spontaneous content. Not to worry, we will discuss the daily management piece at length in chapter 8, but first we have to start at the beginning - building good content.

There are a growing number (7+) of content types compatible on social media platforms overall. The content type, however, varies per platform. Some social media sites offer a slightly different spin to the content they allow as a part of their differentiation strategy, offering features that users are unable to use other places. For example, SnapChat allows you to use photos and videos just as you can on other platforms, but they include a sense of urgency in that you cannot revisit the content an unlimited amount of times as you can with a Facebook or Instagram.

Some social media managers see imagery as the focal point of the post. It is commonly found that most brands notice that posting content with some visual element performs significantly better among their target audience, producing higher engagement than content without it (i.e. text-only). There are times when text-only is needed or useful, but the majority of posts should always have a visual component.

Although visuals are important, there are several other areas we look for content to cover; it needs to be engaging, tell a story, or include a call to action. But, more critical than the visuals to support the content and the post elements we will review in depth shortly, it is crucial that the content is **relevant** to your target audience. Without relevant content, you could produce content up to your earlobes daily but your audience interactions would not positively reflect the work done nor increase the profit and purchase conversions for the brand.

Let's discuss the types of content and applicable uses a little more, and then we can delve into post elements. There are five main content types used currently across the most popular platforms: text, links, photos, GIFs, and videos. Here is a summary chart of content types with the description and the high level use. Following the chart is a breakdown of each area with detailed descriptions and usage. Please note, these can be used together to generate more dynamic content!

Types of content	What is it?
Photo	Visual representation of the text used in a post
Video	Ranging from 15 seconds to unlimited based on social platform of choice, videos engage your audience audibly and visually
GIF	An animated motion photo, much shorter than a video and not including any sound. Often holding a caption to state the sentiment that is expressed visually
Text	Text-only posts simply feature the message without additional graphics or visual support
Link	An active link a user can engage via a 'click' and connect to a page online to view additional content, register, etc.
Others	Additional, platform specific post types are available and offer an alternative version of the content above.

Photos:
Photos are the most common visual support for posts on social media. The medium extends to nearly all platforms and engages the viewer differently from any other content type. Photos tell a story without requiring the user to read, or at least that's how they generally view content with photos. They are easy to share and save, allowing viewers to become brand advocates and influencers among their friends or other users. Most platforms allow photos except video-only ones such as Vine, Vimeo, and YouTube. To circumvent this requirement, users often place music behind a series of photos for an iconographic video.

Photos are especially helpful for platforms like Instagram (you cannot post on this platform without either a photo or video; text-only is prohibited), where you are not allowed an engagement option of reposting within the app. For viewers to be brand advocates by sharing the content is a little more complex on this platform. Instagram is a mobile-only platform and other apps offer the integration options (add-ons), to allow users additional functionality like "reposting." Instagram also does not allow users to 'save' or 'share external' as you can on platforms such as Facebook. A simple screenshot or launching on a desktop version that is "view-only" for the platform and saving it the old-fashioned way are the only options for users to take your post from one platform to another or onto other mediums like text or email, if the user likes it enough. Although rather involved, photos combat this arduous process because there are options, unlike a video posts on Instagram, where the viewers is left with fewer options to share the content.

Delivered in a variety of ways depending on the brand, photos have very few limits. Some platforms dictate the optimal size for the various photo types they allow, or restrict how long the viewer can see the photo before it disappears, but currently that is the extent of the restriction types. The strategic options for how to use photos are endless! Some brands choose to share photoshoots of the product or service, loosely related images to their product or service, behind the scenes shots, sneak peeks photos, collages for a mix of all, user submission competitions, photos generated with text for client testimonials, infographics, and the most popular strategy from a user perspective- memes.

The photoshoots can be done professionally and are usually more successful from an engagement standpoint if conducted at a professional level. Sneak peek, behind-the-scenes and user submission competition usually do really well once you have developed an engaged following. Infographics are images that bring reports and statistics to life. They include charts, graphs, and very detailed information in an organized yet visually intriguing way. They usually include a visual description of the statistics discussed as well. Infographics are a fun way to tell a numbers-driven story.

Memes are a repurposed image, often taken from pop culture, and reassigned a new sentiment purely derived from the image and separated from the original meaning. Memes generally pull together an element from movies or television shows into a photo and the new meaning attached, matches the visual sentiment displayed. Often the connection is expressed via a text overlay on the image. The original image, context and message from the source has no connection with the expression intended when repurposed, but makes a point of a related sentiment portrayed visually. They often hold a comparison of sorts, the unsaid association or thought as perceived a majority wishes to convey or hold an air of sarcasm to which the intended audience would relate.

Example:

*Jackie Chan is a well-known actor, but this image is taken from a movie. In that movie he said nothing about social media but the expression on his face now matches the caption and sentiment of 'why social media'.

When posting photos that are not memes, it's still important to keep a few things in mind:
1. Make sure the photo is in focus and can be seen accurately in the feed (without requiring viewers to click)
2. If the photo is a visual to supplement text providing viewers with information, be sure to place all needed information within the photo
3. See the resources page in the appendix for sites to help build photos and optimal sizes per platforms.

Videos:

Videos are a little bit trickier, although they engage the audience very well (when played), there is a lot of production value to consider. Most brands want a very well-polished and professionally produced product to share. Traditionally, that would be the case across the board. However, with the rise of smartphones, the increase of content demand plus the decrease of interest due to information overload and the oversaturation of viewers, the most important aspect is *relevant content*.

A video of ice being poured on someone's head can go viral and ultimately does better than a $30,000, 30-second commercial. The difference here is the story behind the video and being told *with* the video. I am NOT saying make bad videos and put them out to be successful, I am saying to put care into the messages you craft while not being blocked by budget or overwhelmed by possibilities. Authenticity is what users want. If you are authentic and consistent, you have the first variables of a winning formula!

Similar strategies can be applied from photos to video. Users want content that is entertaining and engaging. A lot of brands use video as an opportunity to explore the culture of their company and establish a connection with users. You might recognize this strategy from the photos section above. The behind-the-scenes photo options are very popular. Videos can also be used for tutorials and how-to education, customer submissions for testimonials and reviews, preview or broadcast an event, share industry-related tips, and more. This is a perfect time to be creative!

I have consulted with many brands that could have had an explosive video presence, but made it too complicated and cumbersome with the budget needs and made an enormous production deal. It does not have to be that robust. The important part is getting out there - that's what social media is all about! People trust it because they want the authenticity, and most brands don't have the capital to have production level exhibitions in real-time and last minute. This is another place where I suggest doing a combination of both prepared content ahead of time and impromptu. The other important part here is the voice used for the content and brand consistency. Whether it's video or photos, the content has to be continuous with the tone (or voice).

Video-only platforms include YouTube, Vine, Vimeo, and Periscope. YouTube is the most popular, owned by Google, and does not require you limit the time of your production for their platform. They offer detailed analytics, for free, and allow users to subscribe to your channel specifically and the addition of keywords to help people find your content. Vimeo is a less popular version of YouTube that does not offer the audience size and all the bells and whistles. Vine is closer to an Instagram for videos only. And Periscope is a livestream available for 24hrs after filming.

Several other platforms allow you to use video, and users often share videos from YouTube or Vimeo. YouTube videos integrate seamlessly and will play on Facebook without requiring the user to go to another page. This convenience factor is crucial if we want viewers to engage with our content. Platforms such as Instagram and SnapChat restrict the duration of video. Periscope is currently changing the landscape entirely, allowing live streaming in real time. The catch is, the video is only available for 24hrs. Several brands are already mastering how to use this platform to their advantage - live Q&A's are just one way!

Others (GIFs, Events, Milestones, Offers, etc.):
The amount of content in this "others" category is growing by the week. As platforms compete for relevancy and users to consistently use their profiles, they morph. GIFs are very similar to memes, but they move like videos. Unlike videos, however, they do not have sound. Originally a Facebook feature, milestones are posts that communicate something significant from the brand to the viewer. Facebook logs it as a permanent part of the brand, but some brands transfer this principle of celebrating milestones with their audience with a regular post, just centered on the victory itself. Offers are another Facebook specific feature. In this instance, you can use Facebook to distribute some kind of deal or discount to users. Setting the amount, details, a link to purchase, and capping how many people are allowed to take advantage is all possible. Events is another useful type of content leveraged by users and brands on Facebook. Social media is not only a place where people want to connect, but also look for things to do. Events allow you to market not only to your followers but to people within a certain geographic area and by interest through targeting.

There are a bunch of content types available to users and businesses across social media platforms now, and more will come in the future as technology continues to change. The most important element of developing content is consistency. Consistency of content and voice keeps people engaged. If it sounds like someone else is writing every post, people will see the inauthentic nature of the profile and disengage (unfollow, unlike/unsubscribe or kill your stats by never engaging with the content posted). Imagine you text your closest friend every day, and one day they sound drastically different. How horrible and confusing would that be? You can tell it is not your friend, because you know the way they type and speak, and even their grammar and punctuation habits sometimes. You know someone else is texting you from their phone and you can no longer trust text conversations. That is what happens when a brand breaks their content voice as well. As a brand on social media, you only have one chance and a violation of trust is the fastest way to tank that chance.

Progress Quiz

1. What type of content would best serve your campaign?
2. Visit the resources page in the appendix and try your hand at making visuals to support your social media content.
3. Describe your content voice.

CHAPTER 5: CONTENT CREATION PT. II

Learning Objectives:
I. Discover elements required for optimized, successful posts
II. Unfold balance in your content with the 80/20 Rule
III. Learn to curate content to increase thought leadership
IV. Establish a standard for curating content
V. Learn how to develop a content voice
VI. Dissect social media content and learn to build content

It's very easy to be overwhelmed by social media, which is quite possibly your primary reason for reading this book. There are so many platforms in existence, new ones appear all the time, and the requirements for posting as a business are frankly outrageous - figuring out what to post can be nearly impossible! Managing social media is truly a daunting experience, but it doesn't have to be. We are nearly halfway through the process of developing a strategy to help you master social media for your business. Our next step is to dissect what it takes to develop a successful post.

When putting together a post, you need five pieces to develop strong content: verbiage, a call to action, a link to more information, a visual element, and hashtags. "Why so much in every post?" you might wonder. There is a reason for every element to help make a post statistically advantaged for engagement. The verbiage is the text or copy in the post. This is necessary because a) it includes several of the other elements, b) it helps target specific users, and c) without the copy, there would be no way to connect with the audience. Sure, the pictures tell a story, videos tell an even bigger story, but the text is vital as well. You can swap pictures for video or vise-versa but you can also send content with text-only.

Other fundamental pieces included in the text are a call to action, links, and the most popular - hashtags. Hashtags are a word or word-phrase with the # symbol in front with no spaces in between, i.e. #Hashtags, #DigitalCode #HashtagsIncreaseYourReach. Once the hashtag is included in a post that is published, the hashtag becomes a live link (hyperlink). When a user clicks the hashtag/hyperlink, it takes them to a real-time feed of content where other users have used the exact same hashtag as the post clicked. Hashtags can be a great source of research for this searchability.

Twitter was the first platform to use the #Hashtag but other platforms quickly integrated similar functionality. Now, hashtags can be used across multiple platforms including Twitter, Instagram, and Facebook. Others might adjust to include them in the future, which would only multiply value greatly. We will continue to discuss the usability of hashtags in the next chapter regarding expanding a post's reach.

A post cannot live on images and hashtags alone! A call to action is prompting viewers for engagement. Engagements vary by platform but mainly include likes, comments, shares, and clicks. Shares and likes, or engagement titles, change per platform. For example, on Twitter a share is called a ReTweet. On Instagram, if you "like" a post, you double tap and the heart turns red. If these terms are new to you, be sure you read over the terms in the glossary, they will help you navigate the social atmosphere much better.

Call to actions can include taking votes, registering, answering a question, donating, or asking a question. Links are essential because at the end of the day, as businesses, we are not on social media for our own entertainment - we are there to make sales! One of the best ways to connect people and increase our website traffic is linking posts on social media to the particular place the content is discussing. Content can also link to other sites that prove thought leadership, but more on that concept later.

Aside from the attempt to generate sales, links can connect to articles, blogs, case studies, or whitepapers. Some platforms even populate a preview once a link is connected within the post verbiage. This brings the header and a teaser of the link destination as well as an image. Link shorteners and vanity URLs are very useful here. Most platforms offer users the ability to create a vanity URL. Generally, it includes the users handle, also known as their social media name and is found in the URL after the "/" for the website address, i.e., www.instagram.com/prof.riley.

Link shorteners are an indispensable tool for social media management. Platforms that have a restriction of characters like Twitter, where you are limited to only 140 characters, a cumbersome link such as: http://www.phoenixarisingconsulting.com/#!Constant-Contact's-Small-Business-Supporter-of-the-year/ctsh/563e864d0cf283308331f5c6 is not very functional or visually appealing. By using a link shortener website like bit.ly you can produce a much shorter link to the same location and not require as many characters such as, http://bit.ly/PACaward2015. There are other vendors that offer this service as well. Bit.ly specifically offers analytics so you can see traffic information for clicks and shares.

Now that we know what is needed in a post, it is imperative to establish balance with the content we produce. Although we are on social media to increase sales, it is not a selling platform. As we discussed in Chapter 3, social media is a place to monitor conversation, engage with users and stay top of mind - not to constantly sell. Considering the balance of self-promotion to information that is required, there is a formula-based rule to help social media mangers achieve maintain balance: the 80/20 rule.

The 80/20 rule entails a split of the subject matter for content prepared and posted to social media platforms on behalf of a business. Out of a 100% content posted, 80% is dedicated to an "other" category for industry information, thought leadership, and industry education. The remaining 20% is dedicated to company-specific content, i.e. sales, promotions, social exclusives and company product/service education. This is the 80/20 rule at large, however, to make the 80% more digestible, it is sectioned off into a 50/30 split.

The majority of the 80% is 50% serving the purpose to engage and entertain the audience with relevant content. The 50% of the 80, dedicated to the industry overall, is often used for posts with industry related humor or irony, fact-based education, trivia, pop-culture and current events integration and references, or to ask questions for market research, among other creative initiatives. This section is intended for the information that will keep people interested and engaged with the content.

The remaining 30% of the 80 is committed to exhibiting thought leadership within the business' field. Thought leadership is demonstrated by being a subject matter expert. Why is that important? Thought leadership is proving you know what you say that you know with content rather than education of the craft or testimonials and 3rd party validation. Although those other elements are great, thought leadership enables the reader to validate you, which is much more powerful for them. Thought leadership is providing informational power to audiences and can include curating content from other sources, company produced original white papers, case studies, books, and any other industry related information relevant to your target audience like tips, changes or news.

There is an extremely high demand for content on social media, so much so that it has spawned its own area of marketing - content marketing. Your social media content does not always have to be 100% original. This process is called content curation. Curating content can be complex in that you don't want to highlight your direct competition. You must give credit but also not detract from you or the message and you have to validate that what is being said aligns with the company values and you agree that it is correct for the field and appropriate for your target audience.

For example, if I am working on a week of content where I am speaking about personal branding, I would not select an article to share that prompted lying on your resume because that does not align with my company core values. I also would not select a piece targeted towards Ph.D. candidates, because their job placement search process is different from the average worker, who is my target audience. The content would not be relevant to my ideal client.

When curating content it is important to follow these steps:
1. Review the piece/information to see if you agree with it
2. What is the process for how I must share this information with my following on this specific platform?
   a. Do they have to access another site?
   b. How many clicks will it take them to get to what I want them to see?
   c. Where will their viewing of this information lead them?
   d. Will they have a good user experience or is there spam?
3. Does this information match the content voice and if not does it supplement mine well?
4. Is the originator of this information in direct competition with my business?
5. Will this ignite conversation and engagement?

Once you have completed an audit with these questions, you can better gauge how this content will fit into your overall strategy. The other key idea to a breakdown of content type is the structure of continuous voice. But first you have to craft your brand's content voice. This process requires you to assess how you want viewers to read and interpret. Some brands have content voices that include an educational and teaching spin, some an air of sarcasm and humor, others very casual as if they are friends with their audience and some extremely formal and professional. The voice depends on the company culture and the type of relationship you want to build. Ask yourself or your team these questions, then brainstorm a bit and try to write content in a few of the options before you comment.
- Do they need to know anything about the industry to understand the content?
- Are there multiple sources or arms of our brand (like franchises) that we need to match or customers will also see content from?
- Would our audience understand this voice?
- Is there any aspect of future content we must address in a sensitive manner?

Now that we have the distribution of content and are making progress to define our content voice, let's try our hand at putting together a post. Remember the 5 crucial post elements:
1. Content verbiage
2. Call to action (CTA)
3. Link
4. Photo/video
5. Hashtags

Let's try it! How would we articulate a post informing people to a key change for your industry? (Give it a try below)

What is the change? (Content verbiage)

_____

_____

_____

Where can they go read more about it? (Link)

_____

How can you help them during this transition (Call to action)

_____

Is there an image that captures this change? (This could be from a press conference, an image of what the change will effect, etc.)
*insert as applicable for your platform, describe the image below.

_____

What relevant hashtags should we use? (Consider ones commonly used within this industry. Is there a hashtag specific to the announcement of this change? And I would include a company specific hashtag if you have created one)

_____

_____

*limit hashtags per post, no more than 6
**be very aware of the different versions for the same sentiment, i.e., #ATL versus #Atlanta. The research we will discuss in the next chapter will help determine which version to use.

Let's try another. How would you articulate a social media exclusive promotion?

What is the promotion? Why should they be interested and what problem would this product or service provide to the purchaser? (Content verbiage)

_____

_____

_____

Where can they click to buy or find out more information? (Link)

_____

What do they need to do to get this promotion? (call to action)

_____

Is there a relevant photo or video where you can emphasize the first point and call to action?
*insert as applicable for your platform, describe the image below.

What hashtags would increase the reach of this promotion and are relevant to people wanting this product or service? Are there hashtags for people purchasing this, looking for bargains or promotions?

_____

Now, let's review the two posts you created above. Did you miss anything? What about the #hashtags used? Unsure which ones to use? The next chapter will discuss the research needed when crafting a post and perfecting the hashtag usage. Go to a few of the pages you like and look at their content to dissect it. Do they include a call to action? What about the hashtags they used? Are there multiple hashtags that lead to a similar search result? Is there somewhere they want you to go where they are providing a link? Is the visual appealing or out of focus?

Below you will find two examples of content, can you tell which is good and which needs a bit of work?

Post 1:

I Am ... An Intraprenuer http://ow.ly/3aoUhK

I Am ... An Intraprenuer

Though they share characteristics, intrapreneurship is not the same as entrepreneurship. This can be good or bad, depending on the individual.

DIGITALISTMAG.COM

*Curated content shared of on FB. Although the post could be relevant, there are elements missing. The image is fuzzy, there are no hashtags nor verbiage enticing to click, only the title of the article repeated.

Post 2:

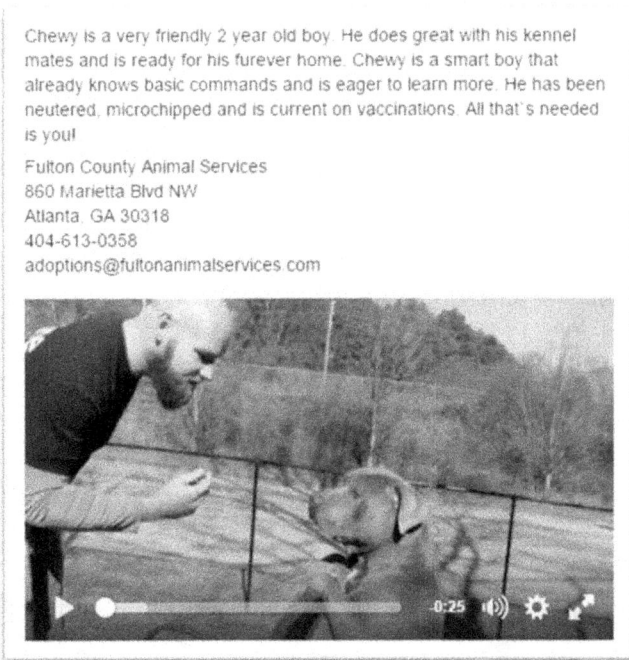

Chewy is a very friendly 2 year old boy. He does great with his kennel mates and is ready for his furever home. Chewy is a smart boy that already knows basic commands and is eager to learn more. He has been neutered, microchipped and is current on vaccinations. All that's needed is you!

Fulton County Animal Services
860 Marietta Blvd NW
Atlanta, GA 30318
404-613-0358
adoptions@fultonanimalservices.com

*Original post included a video, call to action, and prominent information needed for users to engage. Can you find anything missing?

Do you see other changes to be made in the posts? When doing your research to see what other brands post and how they use various platforms, be sure to remember the fundamentals and to add your own creative flare then adjust to your specific brand's voice.

Companies use relevant and optimized content to show their thought leadership and their competitive advantage while engaging with customers to stay top of mind. Thought leadership is a mindset that can be applied to all of your content regardless of which allocation. It's a way to show your expertise in a particular field without just repeatedly stating "we are the best". This approach helps ensure content is relevant to audiences because it is produced entirely to provide additional information on a certain topic of expertise that will help them function better within that area. Content as a whole should be crafted to help your audience in some way, be it entertaining them, informing them or selling to them - it should *always* be customer centric.

Progress Quiz
1. What elements are required for every post and why?
2. How will the 80/20 rule impact your campaign's content?
3. What is the breakdown of the 80% of the 80/20 rule?
4. What is thought leadership and why is it important?
5. Name the research checkpoints for curating content
6. What should one do to help determine their content voice?
7. Try your hand at creating a week's worth of content for your campaign.

CHAPTER 6: CONTENT CREATION PT. III

Learning Objectives:
I. Master an understanding of how to effectively use Hashtags
II. Develop a social media hashtag research process
III. Explore the content sharing cycle

We discussed hashtags in the last chapter but the #Hashtag selection is a completely different ballgame. Hashtags must be researched and crafted with care. Think of them like the cafeteria in elementary or middle school - popularity matters. If you use 16 unpopular hashtags every post, it does you very little good and has no benefit to your visibility. Let's review the research process.

Every business or organization should have a list of approved hashtags for usage in the content they publish. This list develops a go-to place where content generation managers can pull appropriate hashtags that have already been vetted. The research process includes several steps and should be conducted on Twitter, Facebook and Instagram - the three main platforms where people use the feature.

First, we must review the frequency or the popularity of the hashtag and how often it is being used. If we search #digital, and the feed of content that populates with users all using that hashtag is all old posts, we know not to use it. But, let's say the information in the feed continues to change and we see posts from 5 minutes ago to 60 seconds ago - that is a winning hashtag. It is, however, important to consider alternate options to saying the same thing. For example,

#Atlanta vs #Atl - they hold the same meaning, but the results and the people following each will differ. During the research stage, it is fine to log them both as plausible options, but we have to keep in mind to not use each in all posts, only the one that will benefit us the most or help us meet the character limit. Character limits might not be a problem on Facebook or Instagram, but no one wants to read a social media post that is 10 or more lines long.

Next, let's review the meaning behind the hashtag. Is this appropriate for our audience? Will they understand that #TBT means Throwback Thursday or should we just use #ThrowbackThursday? Some brands take trending hashtags regardless of the meaning and use them simply because they are trending. THIS IS A BAD IDEA! Using hashtags without knowing the implied or intended meanings can get brands into trouble. Before using a trending hashtag, meaning a hashtag that is being used in very high frequency and is the latest buzz at the moment, click the hashtag and see what some of the other posts are about. If you cannot figure it out, do not use the hashtag. Another cautionary tale, do not use trending hashtags just to use them because you know a lot of people will see it. The content still needs to be relevant to your audience, and even if you have to spin the post to help the hashtag apply to your goals that is better and more authentic than just including irrelevant information for viewers. Also, if you do hashtag jack like that (that's what it is called), people will know and could possibly lash out against the brand.

Our 3rd consideration during research is timeliness. Outside of trending, not all hashtags are meant for all times. For example, throwback Thursday (#TBT) is usually only done on Thursdays, as is flashback Friday (#FBF), follow Friday (#FF), man-crush Monday (#MCM), and woman crush Wednesday (#WCW). Publishing posts with the wrong day tell your audience you don't know what you are doing, unless you are doing it ironically or sarcastically. Other hashtags are time sensitive or for events. Lots of conferences, shows, and other events have incorporated the use of hashtags to keep people at the event engaged and as a form of generating online activity but also letting those not in attendance to see and follow the action. This process is often regarded as live-tweeting, but is done on more platforms than Twitter. Twitter chats are another application created for Twitter specifically. This is where a brand has a moderator and users can interact in real-time to weigh in on a topic, ask questions, and engage the brand directly during a set window of time. Authors do twitter chats around book launches, and brands and other celebrities participate as well. Users include the hashtag in each post to be included in the feed.

Other considerations and options for hashtag usage include pop culture, location, holidays, and general happenings within the brand organization. The above abbreviations of hashtags are in the pop culture bucket. Holidays such as Valentine's day, Christmas, New Year's day and eve, etc. also have hashtags. It is customary for brands to wish their followers well with a holiday greeting. A consideration here is the religious beliefs of your audience. If your following is primarily Jewish or Muslim, a #HappyHolidays is much more appropriate so as not to insult your audience.

Nailing the hashtag usage is a must for social media content. Be sure to initial cap your hashtag phrases to make them easier to read, for example #UnlockingTheDigitalCode has each first letter of every word is capitalized for ease of reading. The opportunity to use hashtags to monitor competition is also an applicable usage. Everything done with content across the internet is referred to as content marketing. Just as you have keywords when marketing with Google Adwords, and tags with blog posts, hashtags are a means to categorically dichotomize content. The content sharing cycle repurposes content from other digital marketing platforms as a means to streamline information for customers to link them between each place and meet them where they are. The process of posting content in multiple places extends the life of your content but also provides you with more content to post. For example, feature a blog post in an email marketing campaign and the email campaign can then be highlighted on social media. Social is not the only way to build credibility, nor is it quickest way, but it definitely lends to a brand's credibility.

Progress Quiz
1. What hashtags have made it to your approved list?
2. Identify content in other places that can be repurposed for your social media content.

CHAPTER 7: EXPANDING YOUR REACH

Learning Objectives:
  I.   Understand social media's role in search engine optimization (SEO)
  II. Explore the Facebook Algorithm and the flow of content
  III. Define engagement types and discover how that impacts the reach of a post
  IV. Strategically use Hashtags to broaden your sphere of influence

Information overload presents several challenges for marketers and disseminators of content. The biggest difficulties faced are getting found and retaining user's attention. One factor that impacts a business or organization being found in a search online is search engine optimization (SEO). A very complex concept, there are countless books dedicated to understanding SEO. We will not spend chapters dissecting the complexities but instead, let's discuss social media's impact on SEO.

Search engines like Google and Bing operate on an algorithm, or intricate mathematical equation, to produce the results searchers see when looking for information. I like to describe the multifaceted system as the Coke recipe - everyone knows it exists and has their suspicions and speculations, but no one knows for sure all of the factors working behind the scenes (ingredients). Not knowing the equation details or how it runs presents a problem - we are unable to hack it. They do this on purpose of course, what would the world be like if marketers could dictate what results came up in a search?

It would be highly manipulated I'm sure.

We do not know all the details of the algorithm, but what we do know about SEO requirements is directly related to our social media content. The search algorithms look for recent and relevant content (Makes even more sense why it's important to prepare *relevant* content now, doesn't it?). "Why are search engines set up this way?" you may wonder. They pride themselves on being able to produce results people want, matching their search to the best possible options that answer the need for information they expressed with the process of searching in the first place. If marketers were allowed to dictate these results and see the intricacies behind the algorithm, users would become very frustrated and no longer seek information within that search engine. The algorithms behind search engines such as Google are protected for information integrity - giving users what they want, not what we want them to have.

Knowing small details such as the fact that search engines are looking for recent and relevant information allows marketers to rise to the occasion. This is where the thought leadership strategy discussed in earlier chapters comes into play. By populating social media profiles and other web presences (websites, blogs, email marketing, etc.) with relevant content and on a consistent basis, we prove to the algorithm that we should have a place among the search results for topics which relate to us, also known as keywords.

Social media, specifically, helps greatly with the recent requirement for SEO. It is much easier to update a Facebook profile, add a new status on LinkedIn, edit information change on Google+, or post a picture/ video of an event on Instagram than it is to make changes to a website. Websites are somewhat static in that they do not change all the time because your services are just that, your services - they don't change every day. You do not have your web designer altering the layout of the site or your business development team changing the offerings of the company daily. You can, however, post to social media every day, even multiple times a day.

Social media activity allows for brands to prove to Google (and other search engines) that they do what they claim they do.

Algorithms change by search engine, which is why we can "google" the same word or phrase in both Google and Bing and get two different results. Social media platforms are a hotbed for activity; people post things constantly. As a business joining the ranks, you are now among both users and other businesses on the information highway. Posting relevant content that happens to be searched for in a search engine for your specific field helps leverage your company as an industry leader. Without crafting content with a strategy of thought leadership, our competition will appear and your brand will get run over by more relevant information.

This constant activity is one of the reasons a company's Facebook page might appear in the search results over their actual website - it's rumored the search engines seek social media platforms first. Of course, we do not know if that is in fact the case, but feel free to play around with Google and see what types of results you get for keywords in your industry. We do know that Facebook populates many Google search results because they, too, have their own proprietary algorithm.

As one of the oldest social media platforms, Facebook allows a lot of functionality that others do not; not all social media sites have the heightened ability of an algorithm. This capability also affects the way businesses and users interact with the platform. Let's say you have 500 friends on Facebook. On a consistent basis, it is probable that you will only see about a tenth of them on your timeline. This small percentage of your entire list are the only group seen because those are the individuals whom which you engage most often.

Whenever I get to this part in sessions or classes it blows student's minds. So, I'll say it again in a different way - algorithms learn your behavior, and this is why it is so complex. On Facebook, the algorithm is developed to generate content to your news feed that you care about. The best way to deliver information you want is to assess information you have interacted with, then continue to give you content like that or from those sources. Meaning, if I share information with my friends, those friends that interact with me and engage my content (likes, shares, and comments) will see my information on a more frequent basis than those who do not. The only power I have over them seeing it is befriending them and publishing it, so I in essence have no idea whose feed I am a part of on a consistent basis outside of analyzing who is engaging with my content. Once you interact with a new person, add a new friend, or search someone in particular, Facebook then feeds you their information as well, but if you do not continue to engage them, they too begin to diminish from the content feed and are replaced with people Facebook thinks are of higher interest to you.

I might have just blown your mind, and if you are a personal Facebook user, you might feel betrayed, or as my students would say, "played." I encourage you to try it out. Go to your Facebook and search for a friend then scroll down their timeline and like, comment, or share their past posts, then go back to your news feed and you will see a difference in the content you are being served. For those of you not rattled by this news or completely lost because you are just starting your Facebook presence, more information is available from Facebook itself on their algorithm: scroll down, on the right side right under the ad select "more," then "help," and select "newsfeed" and "how does your newsfeed work".

As a business, you want to expand your reach but you also want to touch those that have already subscribed to your content by liking, following, and interacting on your pages. For Facebook, this algorithm affects the content served by brand pages to the fans/followers of these pages as well. If a brand is publishing content to Facebook after the algorithm changes happened, their viewership dropped to about 10% of their likes. Before Facebook added this, viewership was about 30%.

What does this mean for businesses? The more users engage with your content, the more they will see the content. We have to work harder to get people to engage our content. If viewers engage the content (likes, shares, comments) they will see more of our content directly on their timeline. If not, it will not be served to them without paid advertising, a topic to be discussed in the next chapter at length. Additionally, Facebook is always changing, so we have to be alert or follow brands, like Phoenix Arising Consulting, that are knowledgeable and can communicate changes and updates to small business owners. By following social media news, business owners stay in the loop to adjust their strategy accordingly.

At this point some students in my class think, "This is too much, there is no point. Why be active on social at all if it takes all this effort to craft the content then people don't even see it?" Don't fret or become discouraged, there are still plenty of reasons to maintain a presence AND even more ways to get your content to reach your target audiences. The first strategy is engagement prompting content - the more your direct followers engage with you, and the more they will see you. But, in addition to the content, their followers can see some of their activity and their follower's followers as well. This is the viral nature of social media and how content travels through various circles. Let's say we have a large group of friends all connected via Facebook - maybe they went to college together. As friends begin to comment, like, or share the original friend's content, the more their in-common friends will see the post regardless of their frequency of interactions. This is a result of Facebook saying hey, all of these people with this common background or experience (like college) are engaging and interested in this piece of content, let's serve it to other people that have that quality as well.

The second strategy is hashtags. Hashtags can be used to increase the reach of content in many ways. Instagram, Twitter, and Facebook specifically thrive on the usage of hashtags. A company can develop a company-focused hashtag to provide continuity of their past posts. Hashtags that are trending are being used in high demand at the time of them being trending. This helps with reach dramatically. A post including a trending hashtag that is relevant will populate among the results and be seen by countless viewers because the hashtag is being discussed so frequently (how it got to be trending). You can also increase the attention given to the post and your SEO with certain hashtags. If a topic is being searched, regardless of trending status, without a #hashtag it will pull people who are organically mentioning the topic (not as many results), whereas searching for an actual #hashtag will provide profiles of people that used the hashtag itself (resulting in higher proportions and additional exposure).

There are many ways to leverage social media platforms. The third strategy is much more passive. In an information age such as ours, people are constantly looking for information and conducting research. If nothing else prompts you to maintain a social media profile, it should be this. With no profile at all, or an empty one you do not use, those that research you could think anything, be it that you are not as legitimate as you say, that you do not know what you are doing, or that they don't want to do business with you because they couldn't find any information about you. Although things like the Facebook algorithm dictate the way your content is delivered to people that like your page, it does not impact what appears on your page when people visit. I have had clients convert many opportunities because when people researched them they saw the work they were doing on their Facebook page. It can make a world of difference.

Progress Quiz

1. Describe social media's impact on SEO
2. Explain how algorithms effect search engines
3. What is the Facebook algorithm and how does that impact our content?
4. Define social media engagement and explain how that impacts content's reach
5. How do hashtags broaden a post's sphere of influence?

CHAPTER 8: BUDGETING FOR SOCIAL MEDIA

Learning Objectives:
I.   Understand the true cost of social media marketing
II.   Learn the benefits of social media advertising over traditional advertising
III.   Introduce aggregates and their impact on the budget
IV.   Discover various team roles and employment opportunities for managing social media profiles

My students once asked me what metaphor I would use to describe social media. My first instinct was something full of chaos and disorder. The more I thought about it, that comparison seemed inaccurate. Social media feels like chaos if you allow it to overwhelm you. Once you slow down and dichotomize features and functionality provided by each platform and what your target audience cares about, social media is more like a minefield. Why a minefield? Essentially, as a content publisher on social media you are walking through any given platform (posting content) and sometimes nothing happens - you are explosion free. Then other times you take one step (apply social media strategy or tactics) and everything goes BOOM! Social media content is a hit or miss, just like every step in a minefield. The boom is equivalent to your content going viral and generating buzz as it relates to your business. This could be trending on the highest scale or exceeding the page likes with engagement on a small scale.

Although social media can reap unimaginable results, the myth of social media being free must be debunked repeatedly. If you are not in the crowd that has had your bubble burst yet, allow me to bring you into reality. Social media is **NOT** free. Social media is not a magic solution to all marketing. It takes a lot to maintain a social media profile and be successful doing it. We have discussed content curating, content development, content visual enhancement generation, various platforms and their features, and these activities take resources.

An active social media presence will always cost either time or money. The resources needed to manage social media from a financial angle include manpower to manage and an advertising budget. The management perspective includes the content development process, scheduling and publishing posts, actively engaging your subscribers, and content activity analysis. Whether you hire an outside firm like PAC (my consulting firm) or you manage in-house with a team or you are a solo-preneur and you have to do it all yourself, resources are needed to manage effectively.

In addition to the management piece, there are two other financial draws from social media on the marketing budget. A lot of aggregates have a free version but to unlock helpful statistics and engagement analytics you have to access the paid version. This fee can range from $10 per month to $50 per month. Outside of aggregates to manage, discussed more in the next chapter, many social media platforms offer advertising options as well. These advertising options are different from billboards on the highway, they allow you to select your target audience to receive the ads. You are able to select their geographic location, demographic and education information, interests and even hobbies. This type of targeting allows for increase results and strategic advertising over some of the traditional advertising methods where companies were spraying and praying with billboards, radio and television commercials and never knew exactly how people found out about them. The analytics advertising on social media provides solves all of this and proves a return on the investment of time and money.

Developing a social following is all about consistency. To produce content at the volume needed for engagement and the increase of followership, someone has to do the footwork. Building content takes an obscene amount of time and research but, creativity is also needed. Sometimes those qualities are hard to find in the same person. This leads us to the necessity to create a team that some small businesses experience. Copywriters, graphic designers, videographers, strategic planners, data analyzers, customer service specialist and the social media manager to publish and engage users are just a portion of the roles that can be allocated on a social media team. Now, of course, all these roles are not required to be different people but the functionality of the roles must be present in the person responsible for the campaign.

As you can see, a lot of resources are necessary to maintain brand's social media presence, and do so successfully. Research, create, publish, engage, and assess then repeat, no matter how you divide the responsibilities, these elements are far from free.

Progress Quiz

1. Define the budgetary requirements for a successful social media presence.
2. Explain the benefits of social media advertising over traditional advertising.
3. What are some of the team member roles needed for social media?

CHAPTER 9: CAMPAIGN IMPLEMENTATION

Learning Objectives:
I.   Assess the team, resources and determine task assignments
II. Learn to integrate social media campaign initiatives into the overall marketing mix
III. Discover assistance options for efficient daily management

We have covered a lot thus far, but try not to be too overwhelmed. We have our target audience, we are aligned with the company mission vision and voice, we have learned tactics to craft winning content, and now it's time to discuss how we can get all these tasks done effectively. Our first step is to assess the team and assign tasks. We discussed in the last chapter roles that can be filled from a skill perspective. To successfully asses the team we have to be realistic and have time availability and interest as considerations. As the business owner, ask yourself a few questions:

Question 1- What staff members do I have that can help?
If you already have a team, are in a position to get volunteers, or looking to expand with interns, you should consider what role in the campaign will they have. For example, some clients of ours have a nonprofit organization so they have volunteers that can do research for curated content, saving staff members time. Other clients have added interns to the mix for the research and brought us onboard to train them for content generation, publishing and social media management. If you are a solo-preneur or a small team that already has a pretty full plate, are there any possible ways to reallocate

duties or divide and concur? What would that look like for your team specifically?

Question 2- What skill areas is the team lacking that we need to consider outside assistance to supplement?

Even if you have a fully staffed department, sometimes some skills are missing. There is always an option to outsource a percentage of the work. Some companies outsource the visuals to a graphic design team, seek outside assistance developing the strategy from consultants or hire copywriters to perfect the content generation and they manage the dissemination of the content and handle the engagement aspect themselves. These combination options can be friendlier on the budget as you are not outsourcing everything but only portions of what has to be done. Purchasing an all-inclusive package, especially with 100% original content, can be pricey when done right.

Question 3- What tools or resources can I take advantage of to make this process more seamless?

Here we need to identify a list of resources that can be used on a consistent basis to support content generation. This can be websites to generate images needed for marketing, be it memes, company promotional images, or image editing platforms. Resources can also be apps to help with creating or editing photos and videos, as well. Other resources might be aggregates that help with the post publishing process. Since all social media sites do not offer options for scheduling and analytics, some companies elect to seek outside sources. By not having functionality to schedule posts to publish at a later date and time set by you, platforms require business owners to access the platform directly to publish posts which is very time consuming and impractical for most business owners. 3rd party aggregates like Hootsuite and Sprout Social help with this process by offering not only a scheduling solution but analytics as well. See the "resources" section in the back of the book for a list of assets.

Question 4- Are the targeted platforms we have chosen equipped with advertising options?

Not all social media platforms offer advertising options but if the ones you have chosen for your brand or this campaign do, it's a big consideration as to your participation in that optional feature. Advertising can expand your reach by leaps and bounds, and reaching people that you would never have contact with otherwise can be extremely advantageous to your social media efforts. It is critical to have an active profile when advertising so when your page traffic increases, users will have content you want them to see there to engage.

Question 5- What is my budget for social media marketing? Now if you do not have a marketing budget at all, let's start there. Defining a budget does not mean a vendor intends to max out the budget; there will be no judgement or assumptions about the success of the amount allocated. A budget is simply how much you can afford or are willing to spend during a specific period of time. How much should you allocate to spend on social media? There are multiple considerations for what requires money: staff members, outsourcing, advertising, resources.

Identifying a range of money to spend on for these various initiatives every month. For example, if the average is $3,000 per platform for all-inclusive management but $500 for content development without management and your budget is $750 and you have one staff member that can manage the content, it might be best to have a firm prepare content, increase the staff members pay marginally, and allocate some of the funds to paying for a 3rd party aggregate and advertising using platforms.

Now that we have a realistic viewpoint of the resources we have to allocate, we can determine tasks and assign to team members or look for a firm to hire on our behalf. Budget is a big factor for the capacity outside resources will play. Budget also impacts what 3rd party aggregate the company can purchase to help with daily management of the platforms. Not all aggregates offer all social media platforms, so there is a bit of research needed here as well.

After determining the allocation of resources, identifying the budget etc. developing a scheduling strategy is the next step. Different platforms require fluctuating frequencies so identifying how much your brand will post to each platform on a weekly basis is key. Every post must to be treated specifically for the platform to which they are sent. For example, a post prepared for Facebook will not work if automatically sent to Twitter due to the character limit. Neither of them will work for LinkedIn without format changing since both of those platforms allow hashtags and LinkedIn does not. At the moment, a leading reason to not send a post from an aggregate to all enabled platforms is how a post will look without hashtags being functional, in addition to it not being optimized for all platforms at once. Using the same content across platforms is fine, but the format changes must be taken into consideration and the proper adjustments made.

As we fine-tune our crafted messages to adjust to platform features, the next step is to integrate the social media campaign into the rest of the marketing mix initiatives. Combining traditional marketing with digital marketing completes the content sharing cycle. The content sharing cycle is the process of repurposing content created or curated by your company via various digital marketing arenas.

As discussed in the beginning of this book, digital marketing extends way past social media. Social media is one of the best ways to pull together all the other elements and promote to a targeted group of people, but don't forget to leverage the other areas. Other types of digital marketing include Websites, Email Marketing, Google Adwords, Google Analytics, Blogging, Banner Ads/Pop-ups, Search Engine Optimization (SEO), Podcasts, Webinars, White Papers, Case Studies, E-books, Online Classes, and Online forums / Discussion Boards. Imagine the power you could harness with all or even some of these mediums working in tandem with the social strategy you have developed throughout this book.

Connecting a blog post to content published as a part of your campaign strategy links the user back to more of your content, furthering your demonstration of thought leadership. But, the content sharing cycle does not stop with digital. Integrating your social media campaign with the rest of the marketing mix extends the execution of the campaign to multiple venues.

Combining traditional with digital extends your reach past the computer or device screen and lets people know in the "real world" to interact with you online. There are events that happen within social users can participate in for offline occurrences such as LiveTweeting. The process of live tweeting happens when a company provides a hashtag dedicated to the event, show, or conference and people actively tweet their experience using the hashtag. Other companies use hashtags to collect contest submissions they market offline for submissions, include their social icons in commercials on billboards and magazine ads. Don't forget to add icons and handles or links to all collateral pieces as well! If you don't let people know you are online, it's hard to continue that relationship with them after offline engagement.

Progress Quiz

1. What are your team needs, team roles and company budget for social media marketing management?
2. How can you integrate your social media campaign with your overall marketing mix?
3. What options fit your company best to integrate resources needed for efficient daily management of social media content and management?

CHAPTER 10: ANALYTICS & REPORTING

Learning Objectives:
 I.   Learn how to turn objectives and goals into deliverables
 II.   Explore social media variables to measure engagement
 III.   Discover the types of reports your company wants
 IV.   Determine how to use data to improve content engagement

Before starting this book you might not have been aware that social media is a tough job that takes a lot of work, and if you already knew that before this book, hopefully I have been able to illuminate some options for you but also solve problems you had or that this book might have introduced with the "campaign theory". Part of the reason everyone flocks to social is because it delivers what marketers have wanted for years in a nice, little, seemingly neat package - interaction and direct connection with customers that you can track. The real story is that social media is nowhere near "little" nor is it a neat package. It is extremely complex and can be very messy, especially when operating without a strategy. Many companies have had to learn this unpleasant lesson first-hand as they underestimated the power of social media and users having an uncontrolled voice. The process of tagging, or adding someone to your post so they get a notification and linking their profile to your post, allows consumers to callout companies directly if they so choose.

After all is said and done - brainstorming and strategy fleshed out, content generated and published, consumer engagement occurred, interactions posted, responses made and the campaign has been completed - we get to the fun part: reviewing, reporting, and analysis! Although results on social media aren't instant, and realistically can take a year of constant posting and work, users like social because it is all so instantaneous and immediate, everything happens in "real-time". Customers provide instant feedback for things they love, but more importantly for things they hate. It is important to use this time after the campaign has concluded to process feedback and interactions from customers. It is my suggestion to categorically save these interactions along the way during the campaign. Although it can be nice to have the image of the actual feedback, or thumb through an archive of engagement on your page, we all know the black hole effect social media can have. You set out to answer a few questions or check one thing and hours later you have done nothing you set out to do, much less anything productive. To avoid this, during the campaign create an Excel spreadsheet where you can house information like this in a text format rather than image.

Other important notes to take during the campaign is what types of content people respond positively towards and what ignites a fire to get people's interactions flowing. You will also want to take note of the timeframe for engagement to help you determine the optimal time to post, i.e., if you post at 3pm, does it take people until 9pm to engage your content? These factors are crucial for improving the company's social presence for the campaigns to follow. If you are reviewing and tracking these pieces during the campaign, you can also adjust in real time for better results.

We spoke about 3rd party aggregates earlier. In addition to providing a scheduling and automation solution, some of them offer features such as indicating the optimal time to post for your specific audience of followers. Optimal indicates that based on users past behavior, they are likely to do be active online and engaging posts during this window of time. This is also helpful because you do not have to manually track and observe your audience's behavior. Aggregates are an excellent way to avoid getting sucked into the social media black hole, save some time, and prove results.

Automate as much as you can in regards to your social presence, as long as you don't automate content. There are tools that will send a new follower on Twitter a direct message welcoming them - this is the good automation. If you do automate your content, be very intentional with the execution. Do not automate replies, this has gotten many brands in trouble because machines cannot grasp context and underlying meanings and may send inappropriate replies. Also, make sure to research the hashtag you are using before you post. I know this was said before but it cannot be said enough. A popular brand once used a domestic violence hashtag to promote their pizza, not knowing it was linked to a case of domestic violence. Most users can tell when a brand has their social media presence on autopilot and lots of companies have gotten in trouble with that process. Once something goes live and is published, it is VERY hard to recover.

After you fine-tune your content strategy and review interactions, you need to decide what analytics are important to the decision-makers within your company. Do you care about the amount of followers or is engagement more imperative to the success of your brand? If engagement is what matters most, there are key pieces of information to log. Mentions, impressions, shares, comments, likes, page visits, clicks, and more, depending on what platform. I know you might wonder, "What are all these things and why should I care, all I want is sales." Remember the seven touches? These all count! They are users actively engaging or being delivered your content. Mentions, shares, comments, likes, and clicks are social media gold. These all mean people like your content and see it as adding value to their life or others in their circle's lives, thus the sharing. Social media feeds are like a newspaper, most people just scroll through for entertainment. Getting people to stop, read, AND engage is a pretty big deal. Celebrate this victory, then replicate it. That is how you grow a social media presence.

Impressions are a little bit different. This means the content was delivered to user's news feed but they did not engage. Viewers were merely spectators and although they might have liked the content or saw it as useful, they did not engage. This is not a fail, it can mean a number of things. The common user on Facebook, for example, does not know about the algorithm. They are not consciously aware that they must engage to continue seeing your content, so they don't. This is why it is so important to prompt interactions with the verbiage crafted in messages.

Once we have determined the variables of data that matter most to us (they should also correspond with the goals and objectives set from chapter 1), we can craft reports and use the data to make our organization better. A lot of 3rd party aggregates offer a reporting option. This generally covers the demographics so you know the audience split of men and woman as well as age distribution. Information like geographic location for country, state, and city are also included, all information that is helpful in targeting and verbiage crafting. You might find that you thought your audience was majority women, only to find out those that have engaged the most this campaign were men. Reports will also tell you a summary of engagement. Did people like posts with links more than multimedia (pictures and video), did people click the links, how was our content shared, and what was our reach? Reach is how many people potentially saw the content. This number is connected with impressions but different, and both are good statistics to know. Reach is the possible number of people reached, impressions are people who were delivered the content.

If you have not included 3rd party aggregates into the budget, platform offerings discussed earlier in the book have a big role here. Some platforms offer analytics directly within them. They might not be as aesthetically pleasing but the data is there and it can be transferred and transformed using Excel, Word, or PowerPoint for review meetings. I would suggest monthly reviews at minimum; those just starting out with smaller brands can do quarterly for a big presentation and review. Do not let the platform activity go on without maintenance, but an all-out conference meeting is not needed every week. I do suggest when conference meetings are planned with other team members to use the time to also brainstorm. As a manager in the trenches with social, sometimes things can slip through the cracks. Bounce ideas around and get an outsider perspective while you can.

Hopefully this book has been helpful in equipping you to concur social media. Please visit the appendix for a glossary of social media terms, frequently asked question section and resources section to help you get started.

Have success stories using the Campaign Theory?
Submit them to us! info@PhoenixArisingConsulting.com
We would love to hear your experiences applying this theory.

A quick recap for the steps to building a campaign;
- ✓ Remember to align with the company vision and mission, and conduct a SWOT analysis
- ✓ Determine a campaign focus and duration
- ✓ Define SMART goals and objectives for the campaign
- ✓ Identify your target audience and build an ideal customer persona
- ✓ Select the best platforms for your brand (including their offerings and where your target audience is)
- ✓ Select the content types that will lead your campaign
- ✓ Allocate resources to content generation
- ✓ Build a content voice
- ✓ Incorporate the 80/20 rule within your content strategy
- ✓ Develop, refine and review content to optimize for your target audience
- ✓ Continue to create original content and curate content
- ✓ Choose hashtags and conduct research to identify the approved list of hashtags for campaign content
- ✓ Determine a content flow between social media and other digital marketing platforms
- ✓ Allocate budget funds to support social media marketing
- ✓ Assign team roles or outsource to supplement skills needed
- ✓ Determine the use of 3rd party aggregates in your social strategy
- ✓ Integrate the social media campaign into the overall marketing mix for offline and other online areas
- ✓ Review and assess campaign successes and areas of improvement to better future campaigns
- ✓ Create reporting and discover ways to apply data results

Although it might seem like a lot, you can do it. Just take one step at a time. Have other questions not addressed in this book or the FAQ's section? We would like to hear those as well.

Go forth and campaign!

Social Media Glossary

♥ - a symbol used to indicate a "like" for a picture or video on Instagram, generated by the "double tap" and remains at the lower left-hand corner of the image. If it has not been selected by the user as a "liked" photo, it remains white rather than red as appeared here. It is also used as an indicator in user notifications, signaling that your photo or video posted has been viewed and "liked" by fellow users.

@ - commonly called the "*at sign*" or simply "*at*", formally known as a "mention", this symbol is used in conjunction with a "handle" on social media platforms to "tag" another user. This feature is limited as a "business" or "brand page" tagging a personal profile to protect user privacy.

- A symbol commonly used on multiple social media platforms known as a hashtag, formally referred to as a pound or number sign. When used on compatible social media platforms, placing the # sign in front of a word or word phrase with no spaces (i.e. #DigitalCode), and this #Hashtag then becomes a live hyperlink that directs the user to a feed of content where other users also including that exact #hashtag in their posts can be found when clicked. #Hashtags are also available to populate Google search results and are the determining factor for "trending" results. It helps others who are interested in a certain topic quickly find content on that same topic.

+1 (plus one) - This symbol found on Google+, is the equivalent to a "like" on Facebook. It is the user interaction of one user telling another user they have a positive reaction or are in agreeance with the original post.

👍 - The thumbs-up symbol is primarily used on Facebook but similarly to the +1 for Google+, this symbol can be located on some websites as a means to "share" that page on Facebook. Natively on Facebook, it is an indicator that a user has "liked" content posted either in agreeance of the sentiment or positive reaction to the message.

Application-Programming Interface (API) - a set of programming instructions and standards for accessing a Web-based software application. A software company releases its API to the public so that other software developers can design products that are powered by its service. For social media this is incredibly important to the management piece. Without a company's openness to release this information, 3rd party "aggregates" would not be able to assist in the scheduling and posting process making for more efficient ways to engage users.

Audience - the online users that have access to view, comment, engage and share social media content posted by anyone at any time.

Avatar - a virtual representation of the end-user. Most commonly used in the video game world but also referred to within social media as a "profile picture."

Analytics - statistics provided to the profile admin for how audiences are interacting and engaging with the page/account. This can include how many users see the content published ("impressions"), user engagement (likes, comments, shares), best time to post, demographics of the audience, geographic details of followers, etc.

Backlink - a hyperlink that links from one website to another. Commonly used for social media to include a link in content that connects back to the brand's webpage. This process can be used to gather social media users generating traffic on your website to promote a specific product or service, allow users to find out more information or prove "thought leadership" with a blog. Also known as an *Inbound Link* (IBL) these links are important in determining the popularity (or importance) of your website to search engines like Google.

Bashtag - the use of an organization's hashtag in a negative or abusive fashion. Also known as hashtag hijacking. In the majority of cases, the hijacked hashtag is one from a corporate marketing campaign and being misappropriated for negative use not aligned with the intentions of the campaign.

Bit.ly - a free URL shortening service that provides statistics for the links users share online. Bit.ly is popularly used to condense long URLs for the purpose of meeting character limits, making links easier to share on social networks such as Twitter. The analytics are helpful for tracking and proving ROI.

Blog - a frequently updated online hub for submissions relating to a variety of topics under a certain umbrella or a solitary specific topic. Similar to a journal or diary, often updated on a schedule, most commonly once a month or every 2 weeks. There are websites that host blogs and some websites host blogs natively as well. One winning feature of blogs is the ability to allow viewers to publish comments on the posts. A secondary feature is guest contributors and links to promote viewer interactivity. Often used on social media sites to "backlink" to the website hosting the blog to generate activity, blogs are at the forefront of generating content to engage the "target audiences."

Boosted Post - a type of paid advertisement on Facebook, a boosted post allows a brand/business page to promote a specific post to reach an audience in addition to their "followers". This type of advertisement extends the reach and increases the lifespan of a given post rather than the organization go through the process of creating a separate, more general ad. All ads on Facebook can be defined for a given "target audience" that will see the ad in their "mini-feed."

Bots - (Twitterbot) a program used to produce automated posts on "Twitter" another feature includes the ability to automatically "follow" or "DM" users.

Brand Page - some social media platforms offer the ability to have a "business page" separate from personal profiles available to users. Business pages or brand pages come in all forms, and are not only limited to a business. A phrase created specifically for Facebook as their business pages have a variety of classifications including teacher, artist, musician, organization, nonprofit, etc.

Buffer - a 3rd party aggregate used to engage and publish content on user's behalf. Offering both a free and paid versions, the aggregate offers a variety of benefits not normally available natively on social media platforms such as scheduling posts, determining the optimal time to post based on your specific follower/fan audience, edit images, link shortening and analytics. The aggregate is currently compatible with Facebook, Twitter, Google+, Pinterest, and LinkedIn.

Business Page - very similar to a brand page in that business pages offer companies and organizations alike the opportunity to present their brand on a social media platform separate from a regular personal profile. The business/brand pages offer different functionality and additional features exclusive to them and not available for personal profiles generally. These features vary based on platform but can include scheduling, analytics, page managers, targeted messages, events, and advertising to name a few. Platforms that currently offer this distinction include Facebook, LinkedIn, and Pinterest.

Call to Action - a prompting phrase enticing viewers to engage a specific post by clicking, sharing, liking or commenting resulting in a given action to benefit the original publisher of the content piece.

Campaign - a plan to market a specific initiative to a set of users you intend to patron the initiative. This could be a certain event, fundraising, a new product launch or a product push, promote a presence on a new social platform or simply general marketing for increased reach and brand recognition.

Characters - terms used in any given post on all social media networks. This includes letters, numbers, and punctuation. Certain sites such as Twitter have a character limit per post or "tweet" sent out.

Circles - clusters of a user's connections on Google+. Users are meant to create classifications (circles) to group certain people together based on the tag applied.

Circle - given classification on Google+ such as colleagues, college friends, family, etc. When sharing content, a user can limit which circle received an update thereby choosing what set of circles has access to the information.

Clicks - the main engagement on social media platforms, a click, is performed when a user viewing online content selects that content to find out more or see something that is not available in its entirety initially by the preview.

Comment - a social media engagement that includes a public response to content. One of many means for a user to interact with a post, the comment, allows users to not only engage with the publishing party but also each other.

Connections - the LinkedIn equivalent of a Facebook 'friend'. As a professionally centered social networking site users connect with others that they may know but on a professional level. Connections, like friends, have to be mutually approved.

Content - the written, graphic or video information of which social media posts are comprised. Content includes a "call to action", "hashtags", and any other critical information viewers would need to elicit a response for engagement.

Copy - text generated to market a company or specific cause, often by a copywriter. This text can be used for email marketing and is commonly found on websites. Directly connected with "SEO", copy included in content is critical to digital marketing. Copy is used for both online and offline marketing.

Cover Photo - an image that stretches across the entire span of a specific social media page. Normally found at the top of the profile page, above the "avatar" or "profile picture". Like your profile picture, cover photos are public regardless of privacy settings. Cover photos are available on Facebook and LinkedIn for both business pages and personal profiles.

Cost Per Click (CPC) – "search engine marketing" method where the purchasing entity is billed by the number of times a visitor clicks on a banner instead of by the number of "impressions". Cost per click is often used when advertisers have a set daily budget. When the funds spent have reached the advertiser's budget, the ad is removed from the rotation.

Demographics - factors that make up audience details that bring the individuals together and set them distinctively apart. Population details such as age, race, sex, economic status, education, income, employment, among many others.

Direct Message (DM) – a private post sent directly from one user to another or a group of users. This type of message is used to communicate on primarily Twitter and Instagram. Although known by other names on more platforms, nearly every site offers a private message feature.

Do It Yourself (DIY) – a popular #hashtag used on social media commonly for projects done in-home rather than hiring professionals or purchasing the project already completed. DIY projects are often home related and of a creative nature.

Emoticons - originally generated by "characters" put together to be a representation of a facial expression such as :-) (a colon, dash and left-facing parenthesis; representing a smile). These various combinations of keyboard characters are often used in electronic communications to convey the writer's feelings or intended tone. Now many social networks have branched out to providing animated emoticons both stationary images and moving GIFs. On Facebook specifically they come equipped with a "feeling" emotion as well when posted by a user in a status update.

Engagement - a user's participation with a brand's content on any given social network. Typically, the interactions brands consider engagement include audience actions such as likes, double-taps, +1's, retweets, shares and comments to measure user interest in content they've published.

Event - live webpage available to the public where audiences can RSVP, purchase tickets, find out information such as time date and location. Facebook users viewing events are also allowed to post comments, pictures and engage other guests and view the guest list provided the admins settings allow them to do so. Other players in the space include Eventbrite and Eventspot but they do not offer the connectivity Facebook has delivered.

Existing Customers - consumers that have a current business relationship with the supplying vendor of goods or services. Generally this individual will overlap with the primary or secondary target audience of the company or organization.

Facebook - a social networking website that allows registered users to create profiles, upload photos and video, send messages and keep in touch with friends, family and colleagues. Available in over 37 different languages, Facebook includes features such as personal profiles, business pages, a marketplace, online game integration, event management and promotion, groups and advertising. To date, Facebook is the most robust social media platform.

Fan - a social media user that has elected to "like" or "follow" a brand or business page. Generally "fan" is most commonly used on Facebook as that is the place of origin within the social environment.

Feed - an algorithm-generated flow of user published content users have subscribed to by either "liking", "following" or "friending" the publisher. This information is populated into the main page of navigation on the given platform aka the "feed". Advertising also appears on the feed.

Follow Back - an exchange between users on any given social media platform where one user "follows" or "subscribes to" another's feed of information and in return the initial user follows the other as well. Also known as a popular hashtag (#FollowBack) which can thank or request a user to follow their page.

Follow Friday - a popular hashtag and show of appreciation, #FollowFriday commonly known as #FF is a shout out where you "tag" other users to refer your followers to engage or follow them. It is a gesture of recommendation and often generates more followers and social media good will among your followers.

Follow - an action users take on the social networks to subscribe to the entity of which they are following's published content to be populated to their news feed.

Follower - a social media user or blog viewer that subscribes to receive your published updates on their minifeed or news feed.

Foursquare - a local search and discovery service mobile app which provides brick and mortar search results for its users. By taking into account the places a user goes, the things they have told the app that they like, and the other users they have indicated an element of trust for, Foursquare provides recommendations of the places to go around a user's current location.

Friends - a connection status for Facebook personal profile users. A feature not available for a business or brand page, both parties must agree to become "friends" before a connection is made. Quite a few features are available for personal users as "friends" that are not available for businesses using the platform.

Geo-Tag - adding a location to your published post (geolocation or "checking in") tells users subscribed to the original publisher's content where they were when the information was posted.

Google Analytics - a free service from Google that enables web masters and site owners to freely access website analytics data. Google Analytics tracks visitors through your site and also tracks of the performance of your marketing campaigns and conversions as set by the administrators.

Google+ Badge - a variety of branded symbols that can be found on websites to allow users to share the page on their Google+ profile with followers.

Google+ - a social network from Google, the platform shares some common features of other platforms. The most distinct difference being the "circle" feature. Users, business and personal alike, can share messages, links, images and videos with other users. You can also video chat with the 'Hangout' application, or you can upload and organize photos using Google Photos. Since the network is directly connected to Google, the platform increases user's searchability.

Groups - a feature that allows users to come together in a subset to have a separate forum among multiple users. This forum allows for both a closed and open option where users can post documents, publish and reply to posts, manage events as well as create polls.

Handle - a user's social media "name" or alias they choose to represent themselves on a given network. To interact with another user directly with a "mention", a user must put the @ symbol adjacent with their handle. Once done, similar to the hashtag, the name becomes a live hyperlink and the "tagged" user then gets a notification of the published post. @Prof.Riley for example. The handle is also the link used to connect directly via the URL bar for example the URL, www.instagram.com/prof.riley takes a user directly to my profile.

Hashtag - a symbol (#) commonly used on multiple social media platforms that when used on compatible social media platforms, turns the word or word phrase into a live hyperlink that directs the user to a feed of content where other users also including that exact #hashtag in their posts can be found when clicked.

Hootsuite - an 'aggregate' or social media management system for content and brand management. The system's user interface takes the form of a dashboard, and supports social network integrations for Twitter, Facebook, LinkedIn, Google+, LinkedIn and others. The 'API' allows Hootsuite to post to the social networks on a user's behalf to avoid logging into each given platform to engage, post or repost content. Most aggregates, Hootsuite included, allow for the user to schedule content to publish at a certain time allowing a sense of automation to the management process. There are a paid and free versions both holding access to different features.

Hyperlink - an active and live link, offering functionality that when clicked the user or entity that has selected it is taken to a specified location on the internet. The act of 'clicking' allows a user to access the URL that has been embedded by the author and follow said link. For social media, 'hashtags' turn into hyperlinks and allow users to engage with the content by clicking. Website links included in posts also offer this same functionality in conjunction with 'link shorteners'.

Impression - an indicator to social analyzers that the content created has been delivered to the given audience it was intended for. This does not mean they saw nor engaged with the content but that it was populated to their feed and the user scrolled past the post. A useful statistic to ensure and gauge the delivery of your messages to your intended audience. Not all messages sent out are delivered to your entire fan-base due to the 'algorithm' run by many social platforms.

Influencer - a social media person or personality that holds influencing power for other users. This is a user that is sought out by brands to endorse or represent them by posting mentioning them, sharing their content or reviewing the product/service. Their following or 'klout' carries weight in the social arena as people look to them for advice on what to purchase.

Instagram - a mobile-only social media platform owned by Facebook created for photo-sharing originally. The social network also allows video-sharing and photo editing via 'filters' to make images look more aesthetically pleasing as well as video clipping to meet the 15sec maximum time requirement. Also serving as prime real estate for #hashtag usage, posts using this platform do not feature a character limit and can seamlessly be sent to other platforms, such as Facebook, Twitter, Tumblr and Flickr, at the same time.

Interaction - very similar to 'engagement', interactions are based specifically on the shared content in question. It relates to the number of likes, comments and shares combined. Any post has a variety of engagement elements and all of those elements combined includes audience interaction with the post.

Klout Score - a number from 1 to 100 that represents a user's influence via social media. 'Influencers' often have a higher score than the average user. The more influential you are, the higher your score. Adding more networks, increasing followers, frequency of posting etc. all add to the user's score.

Likes - an interaction users and businesses are afforded on the social network Facebook. This type of engagement occurs on a post or page and allows the viewing user to indicate to the original posting user they viewed and hold a positive sentiment for or are in agreeance with the post. Users operating the platform for personal use often use this as a method of interacting with other users without including actual commentary. For a business, however, likes are a means of collecting subscribers. A company that desires more 'likes' is looking to increase their subscribers to their page meaning the users who have performed this action will now see their messages on their 'mini-feeds'.

LinkedIn - a social media platform designed specifically for the business community originally. Very similar to Facebook in the interface of users, but LinkedIn is solely professional. Registered users establish a page synonymous with a resume to brand themselves and their past professional experiences. A site to brand themselves, companies can also have a company specific page on the platform but it is connected with a personal page and does not allow 'connections' and only the option to 'follow' as a means to subscribe.

Mark Zuckerberg - owner of the social media network, Facebook.

Mention - social media interaction including the '@' sign followed directly by a user's 'handle' or social media username. The original poster 'mentions' another user as a form of engagement on a post, highlighting them to give credit, bring attention to content or as a form of acknowledgement and thanks.

Mini-Feed - a key requirement to a functional social media platform that allows users to see all posts by their friends/connections/followers etc. (although subject to the algorithm) in addition to posts from brand pages to which they have subscribed. This feed is where the majority of the engagement and content interactions take place including likes, comments, sharing etc. Also known as a newsfeed, this is the place where users scroll to see new content posted and serves as the main page on a social media platform for users.

Modify Tweet – also known as a 'quoted tweet', this indication tells users you added information to another user's original tweet rather than simply 'RT'ing'.

Myspace - a social media site that allows its users to create webpages to interact with other users. Features allow users to create blogs, upload videos and photos, and design profiles to showcase their interests and talents.

Newsfeed - the homepage of a user's account on a social media profile, also known as the 'minifeed'. This homepage is where all the latest updates from any page or user to which you are connected can be found. Known by a variety of names per each platform, the newsfeed serves the same purpose regardless of platform-specific title, i.e. the news feed on Twitter is called Timeline (not to get confused with Facebook's Timeline which is a user's specific post history).

Ow.ly - a link shortener tool allowing users to enter a full URL and get a shorter URL with the option for a custom extension.

Pay per 1000 Impressions - is an Internet advertising model used on websites, in which advertisers pay for the number of times an ad is show regardless of whether the ad is clicked on or not.

Pay Per Click - an online advertising model where a company that has placed an advertisement on pays a sum of money to the host website when a user clicks on to the advertisement.

Personal Profiles - some social media platforms offer a business specified profiles, personal profiles are the user side of those platforms where users can be active, often featuring different functionality from the business pages.

Pin - a piece of content shared by Pinterest users.

Pinterest - a social networking site that lets people share images and videos from their own personal media collection or from websites they visit. They use a system of "boards" which is a collection separated into categories you choose as the user.

Pixel (px) - a concept derived from the combination of picture and element, a pixel is the basic unit of programmable color on a computer display or in a computer image. Optimal image sizes for social media are measured in this metric.

Post - a published message on a social media network.

Potential Customers - someone that is interested or qualified to purchase the products and / or services of a business.

Profile Photo - very first picture displayed at either the top left or top right corner of the social media webpage from the profile page. Usually the acting photo always representing your profile on all pages of activity with a thumbnail version.

Profile - the webpage of a social network user that displays any content that the user has shared. It is the equivalent of their account on any given social media platform.

Promoted post - a boosted post on social media functioning as an ad but including in the regular feed of content for users regardless of their settings.

Real-Time - method of indexing content being published online with virtually no delay. Activity happening on social media right then and now.

Recommendation - a LinkedIn specific term indicating another LinkedIn user has provided a written endorsement of their working relationship or projects.

Referrals - a process to increase word of mouth marketing by encouraging customers and contacts to talk as much as possible about a brand or product.

Reply - a message sent using Twitter in response to a tweet or mention someone has sent. Also a message sent back on other platforms in response to messages sent to you, your page, or the inbox.

Return on Influence (ROI) – the return of effort built with your social content that has developed a following and has influential power or klout among followers. Different from return on investment, this ROI leverages the relationship built rather than the sales derived from efforts.

Return on Investment (ROI) - an accounting formula used to obtain an actual or perceived future value of an expense or investment. This ROI proves the investment of time or money impacted the bottom line and resulted in financial gain for the company or organization as a result of efforts made.

Retweet (RT) - the act of re-posting someone else's Tweet. Twitter's Retweet feature helps you and others quickly share content that you might find interesting, informative or funny with all of your followers. It is a digital means of cosigning a sentiment sent from other users.

Search Engine Optimization (SEO) - the process of getting traffic from the "free," "organic," "editorial" or "natural" search results on search engines. Maintaining optimized content so your brand appears in an organic search in response to keywords also present in your content.

Search Engine Marketing (SEM) – the process of advertising your digital presence within search engines to increase sales and website foot traffic due to the increased viewers by appearing higher on search results as a result of the promotion.

Share - an action that allows someone to publish content from another source. The content is "shared" from the original location to that sharing user's personal social network or selected pages and viewers.

Social Media - a variety of Web-based platforms, applications and technologies that enable people to socially interact with one another online.

Sponsored Post - also known as a promoted post, is a post on social media platforms which is explicitly sponsored as an advertisement meant to draw a large amount of popularity through user engagement, clicking or downloading content.

Sprout Social - a social media management and engagement platform for businesses, enabling social communication for business through three main functions: publishing, engagement management services and reporting & analytics.

Target Audience - a particular group of people, identified as the intended recipient of content or advertisement. Also called target population.

Targeting - specifically crafting information for your target audience where you know they will receive it in the way intended.

Text-lingo - commonly used shorthand acronyms with longer meanings such as "smh" for "shaking my head" or "brb" for "be right back". These abbreviations are used by people around the world including social media to communicate with each other.

Thought Leadership - is providing informational power to audiences whilst proving you are an expert in your field. This process can include curating content from other sources, showing your team is well-researched or supplying company produced original white papers, case studies, books etc. and any other industry related information relevant to your target audience like tips, changes or news.

Timeline - the space on your profile where you can see your own posts over time, organized by the date they were posted on Facebook specifically.

Trending - a term often used for popular viral topics; it refers to the most popular subjects being discussed by users within a geographic region at a given time, often manifesting as hashtags.

Tumblr - a website that lets you effortlessly share anything. Post text, photos, quotes, links, music, and videos from your browser, phone, or desktop. It is a hybrid between a social networking site (like Facebook and Twitter) and a blog. People usually post short snippets of text and quick snaps as opposed to longer diary style entries found in more traditional blogs.

Tweet - a post or status update on Twitter.

Tweet Deck - a social media dashboard application for management of Twitter accounts. Like other Twitter applications it interfaces with the Twitter API to allow users to send and receive tweets and view profiles as well as schedule content.

Tweeters - people who use the social networking service Twitter.

Twitter Chat - a live Twitter event, usually moderated and focused around a general topic. To filter all the chatter on Twitter into a single conversation a "hashtag" is used. A set time is also established so that the moderator, guest or host is available to engage in the conversation.

Twitter Sphere - postings made on the social media website Twitter, considered collectively

Twitter - Twitter is a form of microblogging. It is about broadcasting daily short burst messages to the world, with the hope that your messages are useful and interesting to someone.

Twitter-verse - a term used for all the users and comments on the social networking site, Twitter.

Unlike - changing your mind about "liking" a post or page and reversing the initial "like" status. This could be due to spam, un-related interests, inappropriate content or posting too much etc.

Unsubscribe - to cancel a subscription to or remove a name from an online mailing list, publication, social media profile or service.

Uniform Resource Locator (URL) – a website address

Vanity URL - a customized web address that includes the name of your business for marketing, branding, and search engine optimization (SEO) benefits. They are usually short and descriptive, and can easily be recognized as part of your business's branding.

Verified Account - used to establish authenticity of identities of key individuals and brands on Twitter and Facebook. They concentrate on highly sought users in music, acting, fashion, government, politics, religion, journalism, media, sports, business and other key interest areas.

Vine - a popular video-sharing app for smartphones where you can share I wide range of content. Each video on Vine can only be six seconds long. It is also referred to as a looping video app (because the video replays itself).

Viral - a growing phenomenon on the Internet where content from small, independent sources briefly catches the attention of a large number of people through indirect means.

Voice - the tone of a user or profile on social media.

Webinar - a live meeting that takes place over the web. The meeting can be a presentation, discussion, demonstration, or instructional session. Participants can view documents and applications via their computers, while shared audio allows for presentation and discussion.

YouTube - a free video-sharing Web site that lets registered users upload and share video clips online at the YouTube.com Web site. To view the videos you are not required to register. Videos include, movie/episode clips, tutorials, DIY's, products reviews and music.

Social Media F.A.Q's

<u>General Social Media</u>
1. *How do you ensure users see the content on your social media page as important?*
    a. Content must be relevant to the subscribing audience. This is why the process of identifying a target audience is crucial in a campaign. If you do not know what group you are targeting, it is nearly impossible to generate relevant content they want to see.
2. *Is it possible to connect all social media platforms so I can just post once and the messages go everywhere?*
    a. There are some 3rd party aggregates that have tried at functionality such as this. As new, thriving social media platforms pop up more and more frequently, it becomes a matter of them releasing their API* for availability to access on a user's behalf. Some companies refuse to do so for a significant period of time and even if they release the API, it does not allow for all the functionality as using the platform natively does. In addition to this, every social media platform functions differently so sending any and all content to them all is not the best idea. For example, a Facebook message is not formatted the same as a Twitter message. The users are different on

each platform and certain features are available on some and not others, like hashtags. If you sent a message full of hashtags to LinkedIn it would look very bad because they do not work there.

3. *If I have active social media profiles does this mean it is possible for me to be "found" with Google or other search engines?*

    a. Most certainly! Anything done online can attribute to the "google-able" nature of a person or topic. Due to the algorithm supporting both Google and social media profiles, specifically Facebook, activity done on social media feeds the recent publishing the system looks for when generating Google or search engine results.

4. *What is the best way to analyze how well a social media campaign worked?*

    a. Analytics provided by the platform natively or analytics produced by a 3rd party aggregate will tell you the stats needed to prove or justify campaign results. On a qualitative side, every campaign needs objectives, these objectives should be measurable and will help evaluate the success of the campaign. For example, if you have an objective to grow your following by 20%, if at the end of the campaign the following has only grown 5%, we know it was either not a realistic goal or another challenge in the campaign execution.

5. *I'm a small business, do I really need a social media presence?*

    a. Yes of course! Now social media not only connects users with businesses, it is also seen as a point of validity builds credibility for a company. In this information age, consumers research more than ever. Due to the viral nature of social media and Google searchability, the more activity a company has the higher the probability the profile will appear when searched.

6. *I've heard social media can validate my business, is this true?*
   a. Yes, in some ways. There are two main elements that give a company credibility, a business card and a website. Once upon a time you needed clients or referrals and a business card. The introduction of the internet added a website and now social media has added a new element. Being active on at least one social media platform helps the credibility of small business owners with clients and Google.

7. *How does the rest of the digital marketing world coincide with social media marketing specifically?*
   a. There are no silos in digital. Everything connects with everything else. The content sharing cycle helps with the dissemination of content across all possible avenues. Posting on social media about a sale on your website, or boosting a post on Facebook featuring the latest blog post or using Constant Contact to get Facebook likes and giving away a white paper, are all ways to connect other areas of digital marketing to your social media platforms.

8. *I want to become a freelance social media expert, where do I start?*
   a. First, you want to start by building a portfolio of content. The easiest way to do this would be to lend your services to organizations like

nonprofits to help them keep up with social content demand or small marketing agencies to help them maintain client demand. Building this content for free can turn into a paid role but also allows you the opportunity to see the process from a variety of vantage points while building your portfolio.

9. *I'm not a graphic designer, how can I make stunning graphics to compliment my social media content?*
    a. Most digital devices these days come with a pretty high class cameras, you can start by learning the options and features with that. Next, visit the resources section of this book. Multiple sites listed there can help you with visual support for your social media campaigns including infographics, memes and edited pictures.

10. *Should I write in the first or third person on these platforms?*
    a. That is completely up to your company, the content voice for your brand will determine which approach you take here.

11. *Is there an easier way to manage all of my social media pages?*
    a. Social media aggregates allow tracking of brands, scheduling content, gathering statistics and engagement reporting etc. These tools in addition to photo editors, content calendar templates and team management apps help make this process more efficient.

12. *I liked a business page but never see anything from them. Why?*
    a. Because you have not engaged with the page! Content is sent out on Facebook all the time and the Facebook algorithm sends the information to page followers. The algorithm

learns what customers do and do not like, if a customer or follower does not engage the content published by the page i.e. like, share, comment etc. Facebook thinks the content is not of interest and stops sending the information to their newsfeed.

13. *I'm trying to post links to content on my website to increase traffic but the link takes up all the characters in the tweet or just looks bad on Facebook, what are my options?*

   a. A URL shortener is your best option to address this issue. Bit.ly and ow.ly are the most popular. They allow you to shorten the length of your URL and even customize the extension at the end but they also gather statistics and analytics for how people have interacted with the link.

RESOURCES

I have gained the knowledge used to write this book first hand by simply working within the field for the last ten years. But, there are plenty of references and resources that can help bring you up to speed even if you aren't a classically trained marketer, you are new to social media or you are in marketing but want to learn how to maximize a social media presence. I hope this list helps, but remember to enjoy the adventure of social media as you embark on this journey!

Meme Creators:
- www.memegenerator.net
- http://memeful.com/generator?ref=9gag
- www.imgflip.com/memegenerator
- www.memecreator.org/create
- www.imgur.com/memegen
- www.imagechef.com/meme-maker
- www.memecenter.com/memebuilder
- http://www.quickmeme.com/caption

Aggregates:
- Hootsuite
- Buffer
- Sprout Social
- TweetDeck
- ZoHo
- eClincher
- IFTTT
- SocialOomph
- SocialBro
- CrowdBooster

Content Calendars, Visuals and other resources:
- Tweetchat
- Storify
- WhatTheTrend
- Flipagram (app)
- PicMonkey
- Basecamp
- GraphicStock
- Canva
- Venngage
- Infogr.am
- Recite
- Quotescover
- Fotor
- Skitch
- Trello
- iWatermark (app)

Resource Hubs:
- SocialMediaToday.com   - HubSpot.com
- SocialMediaExaminer.com   - MarketingProfs.com

Optimal photo dimensions 2016:
Resource- (https://garage.godaddy.com/webpro/design/facebook-profile-picture-size-and-more/?cvosrc=social+network+paid)

    Profile picture sizes-
Twitter profile picture size: 400px x 400px
Facebook profile picture size: 180px X 180px
Instagram profile picture size: 110px x 110px
Pinterest profile picture size: 165px X 165px
LinkedIn profile picture size: 400px x 400px
YouTube profile picture size: 800px x 800px
Google+ profile picture size: 250px x 250px

    Cover photo sizes-
Twitter header: 1500px x 500px
Facebook cover photo size: 851px x 315px
Pinterest cover photo: 217px x 147px (Board cover image)
LinkedIn cover photo: 974px x 300px
LinkedIn story photo: 698px x 400px
YouTube cover photo: (varies by device) 1546px x 423px desktop
Google+ cover photo: 2120px x 1192px

    Shared images sizes-
Twitter: 1024px x 512px
Facebook: 1200px x 630px
Instagram: 1080px x 1080px
Pinterest: 735px x unlimited (Expanded Pin)
LinkedIn: 350px x 250px
YouTube: 16:9 aspect ratio (Video)
Google+: 497px x 373px, but can be as large as 2048px x 2048px

    Shared link graphic sizes-
Twitter: 1024px x 512px
Facebook: 1200px x 628px
Instagram: 238px x 238px (Photo Thumbnails)
Pinterest: 235px x 800px (Preview); 68px x 68px (Board Thumbnail)
LinkedIn: 180px x 110px (thumbnail)
YouTube: 1280px x 720px (Custom Video Thumbnail)
Google+: 497px x 373px

ABOUT PROFESSOR RILEY
Consultant | Professor | Author | Digital Marketing Expert

Professor Jen Riley hails from Atlanta, GA, the headquarters of her consulting firm, Phoenix Arising Consulting (PAC). A partner for small businesses, nonprofit organizations, and entrepreneurs, PAC joins forces to help establish or grow brands with specialty, digital marketing services. Services include Social Media Marketing, Email Marketing, Website Development, Graphic Design, Google Properties Management, and Custom Curriculum Design. Riley has built her career over the last 10+ years in Digital Marketing in corporate America, consulting and teaching college courses and small businesses custom solutions to differentiate their brands.

Prof. Riley is an active member of Toastmasters International, an organization focusing on professional development of communication and leadership skills. She is a proud graduate of Oglethorpe University in Atlanta, GA and received her Master's in Marketing with an emphasis in Social Media Marketing from GA State University. Since college, Professor Riley continues her thirst for knowledge by completing digital marketing certifications and looks to complete her doctorate degree in entrepreneurship.

Text PACINFO at 22828 to join Prof. Riley's mailing list!

www.LinkedIn.com/in/jenrileyms
Facebook.com/Prof.Riley | Instagram- @prof.riley

www.PhoenixArisingConsulting.com

[85]

www.ingramcontent.com/pod-product-compliance
Lightning Source LLC
Chambersburg PA
CBHW071112210326
41519CB00020B/6279